great food
for families

RYLAND
PETERS
& SMALL
LONDON NEW YORK

great food for families

child-friendly food that adults will love too

Fran Warde

photography by Caroline Arber

Dedication

**For my boys, big and little—
David, Otto, and Chad.**

First published in the United States in 2006
by Ryland Peters & Small, Inc.
519 Broadway, 5th Floor
New York, NY 10012
www.rylandpeters.com

10 9 8 7 6 5 4 3 2 1

Printed and bound in China.

Library of Congress Cataloging-in-Publication Data

Warde, Fran.

  Great food for families / Fran Warde ;
photography by Caroline Arber.

     p. cm.

Includes index.

ISBN-13: 978-1-84597-218-9

ISBN-10: 1-84597-218-X

1. Cookery, American. I. Title.

TX715.W23836 2006

641.5'973--dc22

2006015481

Commissioning Editor Julia Charles
Project Editor Patricia Burgess
Production Sheila Smith
Art Director Anne-Marie Bulat
Publishing Director Alison Starling

Food Stylists Lucy McKelvie, Anna Burges-
Lumsden, Alice Hart and Joss Herd
Prop Stylist Clare Hunt
Indexer Hilary Bird

Notes

• All spoon measurements are level unless
otherwise specified.

• All eggs are medium unless otherwise specified.
Uncooked or partly cooked eggs should not be
served to the very young, the very old, those with
compromised immune systems, or to pregnant
women.

• Ovens should be preheated to the specified
temperature. If using a convection oven, cooking
times should be reduced according to the
manufacturer's instructions.

• Health specialists recommend that children
whose families have a history of allergies should
not be given nuts to eat in any form until they are at
least three years old. Children under five should not
be given whole nuts in case of choking.

Author's acknowledgements

Thanks go to my parents for giving me such a
good food start in life. My granny by the sea taught
my mum to cook, my dad bought a lovely house
with a big garden for growing vegetables, and our
family of six all ate freshly prepared food round the
table. It was beautiful and that simple.

Many thanks to Alison Starling at Ryland Peters &
Small, and special thanks to Julia Charles, who has
a voice that sounds like sunshine on the phone.

Finally, a big thank you to Caroline Arber for her
lovely food photography.

contents

6 introduction

12 the best start

32 family lunch boxes

54 quick weekday suppers

68 get-ahead weekends

90 sunday dinner

104 family and friends

120 sweet treats

142 index

introduction

Nothing is more important than a happy
family, and one way of helping to achieve this is
by providing healthy food. Well-fed children are
bright, funny, and good company, and this has
a lot to do with what you feed them. My mantra
is "cook from scratch." Convenience foods might
do no long-term harm if used just now and

again, but I'm convinced that too many people have become reliant on them and are jeopardizing their health in the process. Who wants all the fat, sugar, and salt they're crammed with? Not me—and I certainly don't want it for my family.

Growing children need a healthy, balanced diet, and they need to be part of making the choices that achieve this. So go shopping together and let them help choose the fruit, vegetables, meat, and fish to put in the cart. Play games while shopping, asking them which country various items come from, whether they grow on trees or in the earth, how they can be cooked, and so forth. They can become

really fascinated by ingredients and keen to discover what they taste like. Children who have seen ingredients in their raw state are not suspicious and confused by a new vegetable that is put in front of them: instead, they feel knowledgeable.

When you're back at home, get them to help unload the shopping and put it away. Filling the fruit bowl, for example, will make them aware of what's available at different times of the year, while stocking dry goods in the cupboards will alert them to the wealth of ingredients that go into their meals. Then chat about what's for dinner and ask if they'd like to help with the cooking. Perhaps they could wash the potatoes that are going to be baked, or trim the broccoli. While you're working together you could explore their senses, asking if they can name different foods that are salty, sweet, sour or spicy. Start simply and they will let you know if they want to be more involved.

Children are great at setting the table, and enjoy having their particular areas of expertise. For example, I've noticed that little girls seem to love folding napkins and making placecards when two or more families are at the table, while boys enjoy sorting out the glasses and drinks. Everyone has a part to play in healthy family eating, and it's so rewarding to sit around a table chatting, laughing, and enjoying good home cooking.

I am passionate about good eating habits in people of all ages. Adults too need good nutrition to feel well and function effectively. There's no need to eat a poor and highly processed diet, even if money is tight, and I believe that the recipes in this book prove it. They're full of flavor and color, packed with nutrients, and, of course, absolutely delicious. I hope they will change the way you cook for your family.

the best start

An old saying tells us, "Breakfast like a king, lunch like a queen, dine like a pauper," and there's a lot of wisdom in that advice. It's all to do with giving the body the right amount of fuel at the appropriate times of day. We all know how distracted and irritable we can get on an empty stomach, and how uncomfortable it is to go to bed on a full one. Children have slightly different needs from those of adults because they are growing, but one thing is undisputed: we all need a good breakfast to start the day.

Lots of people say that they can't face food in the morning, but that's no excuse for not giving the body some nutrition to help it through till lunchtime. Smoothies are quick and easy to make, full of energy-giving ingredients, and slip down with no effort. There's a fantastic selection in this chapter, and there are lots of other ideas for light and healthy breakfasts, including fruit compotes, homemade cereals and yogurt, delicious breads and muffins, and that perennial favorite—eggs. There really is something for everyone in these pages.

Smoothies are a great way to start the day. Packed with fresh fruit, their lovely fresh, clean flavors will gently awaken your taste buds. They are also good when frozen and served as freezer pops in the summer. In fact, I know one little boy who will not eat fruit, but loves smoothies, so they're a great way of making sure your family gets the benefit of all the healthy nutrients that fruit contains. If you do not already have a juicer, it's worth investing in one because it makes life easier and you can have fun making up your own combinations of favorite fruits and flavorings.

carrot, apple, and ginger smoothie

Preparation 8 minutes
Serves 2

5 large carrots, peeled
5 apples, cored
1 inch fresh ginger, peeled

The combination of ingredients in this recipe makes it a fantastic pep-up—great to drink for breakfast or when feeling under the weather. Everyone loves it, although children may take a little while to get used to the slightly hot flavor that the ginger adds.

Press all the prepared ingredients through a juicer and serve immediately.

raspberry, kiwi, and blueberry smoothie

Preparation 5 minutes
Serves 2

2 cups raspberries, fresh or frozen (no need to thaw)
2 kiwis, peeled
2 cups blueberries, fresh or frozen
¾ cup milk

Experts tell us that blueberries are great brain food, so blast some together with other delicious fruits and make this wickedly colored smoothie to serve at any time of the day.

Put everything in a blender and blitz until smooth. Adjust the consistency with milk if you wish, and serve right away.

strawberry and banana smoothie with wheat germ

Preparation 10 minutes
Serves 2

about 2 cups strawberries, hulled
2 large bananas
1½ cups milk
4 tablespoons plain yogurt
2 tablespoons wheat germ

Full of fruity goodness, this delicious smoothie also contains wheat germ for extra fiber. It always reminds me of the early morning smoothies I used to drink after swimming at Bondi Beach in Australia. In fact, I think the whole idea of smoothies probably originated Down Under.

Put the prepared fruit in a blender with the milk, yogurt, and wheat germ. Whiz until smooth and drink right away.

mango lassi

Preparation 10 minutes
Serves 2

1 cardamom pod (optional)
2 mangoes
1 cup plain yogurt
½ cup apple juice
1 tablespoon honey
a pinch of nutmeg

Lassi is an Indian drink—a refreshing mixture of yogurt and water. It can be flavored in lots of different ways, but cardamom pods are a traditional addition. This drink is often served with curry to cleanse and cool the palate.

Gently crush the cardamom with a pestle and mortar, discard the pod, and crush the seeds.

Peel the mango and cut the flesh away from the pit. Put in a blender with the yogurt, apple juice, honey, nutmeg, and cardamom seeds, whiz until smooth and serve.

There's no better way to preserve the lusciousness of fruit than in a compote—and it's so easy to do. You can use any seasonal ripe fruit, and it's lovely to have it all year round with muesli, hot cereal or homemade yogurt (see pages 21–22). Compote is also great served as a simple and light dessert after a rich meal. Experiment with combinations of your favorite fruits to make your own particular blend.

winter dried fruit pot

Think of Christmas pudding and this recipe will deliver that intense flavor every morning of the year. The longer you leave it to steep, the more the fruits will plump up.

Preparation 5 minutes
Cooking 30 minutes
Serves 6

¾ cup dried apricots, pitted
¾ cup dates, pitted
¾ cup prunes, pitted
¾ cup golden raisins
1 cup dried blueberries
¼ cup dark brown sugar

Put all the ingredients in a saucepan, add just enough water to cover, then stir. Bring to a boil and simmer for 30 minutes. Let cool, then transfer to a storage jar with a tight-fitting lid and refrigerate until needed.

rhubarb and plum compote

Girls just love this fruit compote, probably because of its vibrant pink color, but everyone enjoys its delicious flavors.

Preparation 10 minutes
Cooking 10 minutes
Serves 6

1 lb. rhubarb, chopped
1 lb. plums, pitted
1 inch fresh ginger, peeled and thinly sliced
⅓ cup sugar

Put all the ingredients in a saucepan with ⅓ cup water, cover with a lid, and bring to a boil. Lower the heat and simmer for 5 minutes. Leave the lid on and set aside to cool. Transfer to a storage jar with a tight-fitting lid and refrigerate until needed.

apple and pear compote

This simple combination is a great introductory compote for young children. Serve on its own or with warm oatmeal, or use as the basis of a crumble.

Preparation 10 minutes
Cooking 10 minutes
Serves 6

1¼ lb. apples, peeled, cored, and chopped
1¼ lb. pears, peeled, cored, and chopped
¼ cup light brown sugar
1 vanilla bean, split lengthwise

Put the fruit in a saucepan with 3 tablespoons water, then add the sugar and vanilla pod. Stir, cover with a lid, and bring to a boil. Lower the heat and simmer for 5 minutes. Leave the lid on and set aside to cool. Transfer to a storage jar with a tight-fitting lid and refrigerate until needed.

Nothing beats a bowl of hot, creamy porridge to get the day off to a good start: it's quick, easy, unprocessed, nutritious, and is digested slowly, so it keeps you going until lunchtime. Always soak the oats overnight as this makes for a creamier consistency. If you're in a hurry, you can make porridge in the microwave: cook on full power for about three minutes, then stir and cook for another minute.

muesli

It's great to be in control of what goes in your breakfast cereal, and this recipe allows you to do just that. For a soft and creamy breakfast, combine equal amounts of this muesli with yogurt and refrigerate overnight.

Preparation 20 minutes
Serves 6

1⅔ cups rolled oats
¾ cup bran flakes
⅓ cup wheat germ
½ cup dried apricots, chopped
½ cup dried cherries
½ cup golden raisins
½ cup flaked coconut
½ cup hazelnuts, toasted and chopped
½ cup pecans, chopped
2 tablespoons sunflower seeds

Combine all the ingredients in a mixing bowl. Store in an airtight container.

granola

This cereal is delicious for breakfast or as a tasty nibble straight from the jar. The more maple syrup you add, the crunchier the mixture will be.

Preparation 20 minutes
Cooking 45 minutes
Serves 4

2¼ cups old-fashioned rolled oats
⅔ cup almonds
2 tablespoons pumpkin seeds
2 tablespoons sunflower seeds
1 tablespoon sesame seeds
1 cup pure maple syrup
¾ cup dried apricots
¾ cup golden raisins
2 tablespoons nonfat dry milk

Preheat the oven to 325°F and line a baking sheet with parchment.

Put the oats, almonds, and seeds in a bowl and mix well. Spread on the baking sheet in an even layer and drizzle with the maple syrup. Put in the oven and bake for 25 minutes.

Remove the baking sheet, add the dried fruit and milk and mix well. Return to the oven and bake for a further 15 minutes, until the mixture is crisp and golden. Let cool, then store in an airtight container.

dairy porridge

Packed with goodness, this is great for growing children.

Preparation 5 minutes + overnight soaking
Cooking 8 minutes
Serves 4

1 cup old-fashioned rolled oats
4 cups milk

Place the oats and milk in a nonstick saucepan. Stir, cover, and leave in a cool place overnight.

The next day bring to a boil, stirring constantly, and simmer for 1 minute. Adjust the consistency with a little more milk if necessary, and serve.

water porridge

This is ideal if you need to lower your dairy intake. You can add a little milk at the table, if you wish.

Preparation 5 minutes + overnight soaking
Cooking 8 minutes
Serves 4

1 cup old-fashioned rolled oats

Place the oats and 1 quart water in a nonstick saucepan. Stir, cover with a lid, and leave in a cool place overnight.

The next day, bring to a boil, stirring constantly, then simmer for 1 minute. Adjust the consistency with a little more water if necessary, and serve.

Calcium is vital for healthy teeth and bones, and eating yogurt is a great way of getting enough. Making your own is really easy, and much more nutritious than store-bought, which is often full of added sugar. It is best to make it in a special yogurt machine according to the manufacturer's instructions, but note that it will be runnier than commercial yogurt, which generally has artificial gums and thickeners added. However, you can make homemade yogurt thicker if you strain it through cheesecloth.

plum and honey cup

When plums are abundant, simmer them and serve with a luscious mixture of yogurt and mascarpone.

Preparation 10 minutes
Cooking 15 minutes + cooling
Serves 4

1¼ lb. plums
2 tablespoons honey
¾ cup plain yogurt
¾ cup mascarpone

Pit the plums and put in a saucepan with the honey and 3 tablespoons water. Bring to a boil over medium heat, then cover and simmer very gently for 8 minutes. Set aside to cool.

Mix the yogurt and mascarpone together. Half-fill 4 glasses with this, then top with the cooked plums.

frozen berry yogurt cup

During the winter months bags of frozen berries provide a lovely taste of summer. Layered up with yogurt, they make a great breakfast or dessert treat.

Preparation 10 minutes
Serves 4

18 oz. frozen mixed berries
½ cup unrefined cane sugar
2 cups natural Greek yogurt

Put the frozen berries in a blender with the sugar and blitz into small pieces. Take 4 glasses and fill with alternating layers of the yogurt and berries. Let sit for 5 minutes before serving.

banana, pecan, and granola yogurt pot

This mixture is always a taste of heaven either for breakfast or at the end of the day.

Preparation 10 minutes
Serves 4

1¾ cups plain yogurt
3 ripe bananas, sliced
⅓ cup pecans
⅓ cup dark brown sugar
¾ cup granola (see page 21)
1½ oz. semisweet chocolate, grated

Spoon some yogurt into 4 glasses. Top with the bananas, then add the pecans, molasses sugar, and granola. Spoon the remaining yogurt over the top, then sprinkle with the chocolate and serve.

It's fantastically relaxing to knead your own dough, but few of us have the time to do so. That's where bread machines come in. They deliver great loaves with very little effort, and you can be certain that they contain none of the undesirable additives found in ready-made bread. Of course, the lack of preservatives means that they don't keep very long, so store the bread in an airtight container or wrapped in the fridge. If you prefer your loaves with a soft crust, put the warm bread in a plastic bag to cool.

whole wheat bread

This is a staple in our house, and a whole loaf can disappear at a single meal. But it doesn't matter, as I just fill the machine again and a little while later another lovely fresh loaf appears.

Preparation 10 minutes
Cooking approx. 3 hours in bread machine
Makes 1 loaf

1½ cups warm water
1 package rapid-rise yeast
1 tablespoon sugar
¼ teaspoon vitamin C powder
4 tablespoons olive oil
2¾ cups whole wheat flour
½ teaspoon salt

Pour the water into a glass measuring cup, dissolve the yeast, sugar, and vitamin C powder in it and set aside for 5 minutes. Pour the liquid into the bread machine with the oil and add the flour and salt. Switch the machine to the whole wheat setting and bake the mixture according to the manufacturer's instructions.

milky white bread

Slightly richer than an ordinary white loaf, and great for toasting.

Preparation 10 minutes
Cooking approx. 3 hours in bread machine
Makes 1 loaf

1½ cups warm milk
1 package rapid-rise yeast
1 tablespoon sugar
¼ teaspoon vitamin C powder
3¾ cups white bread flour
½ teaspoon salt

Pour the milk into a glass measuring cup, dissolve the yeast, sugar, and vitamin C powder in it, and set aside for 5 minutes. Pour the liquid into the bread machine with the oil and add the flour and salt. Switch the machine to the white bread setting and bake according to the manufacturer's instructions.

spiced bread

Enriched with milk, eggs, and butter, this is a lovely teatime treat.

Preparation 10 minutes
Cooking approx. 3 hours in bread machine
Makes 1 loaf

1 cup milk
1 package rapid-rise yeast
2 tablespoons sugar
2 eggs, beaten
1 stick butter, melted
3¾ cups white bread flour
⅔ cup golden raisins
1 teaspoon ground cinnamon

Pour the milk into a glass measuring cup, dissolve the yeast and sugar in it, and set aside for 5 minutes. Pour into the bread machine with the eggs and butter, then add the flour, raisins, and cinnamon. Switch the machine to a fruit bread setting and bake according to the manufacturer's instructions.

These homemade breakfast muffins are full of fiber and goodness instead of the usual load of sugar. They also make tasty lunch box treats. It's worth buying a flexible plastic muffin pan: it does away with the need for fiddly paper liners and produces perfect muffins every time.

oat and apple muffins

Children love helping to make these muffins, and they certainly enjoy eating them.

Preparation 15 minutes
Cooking 30–40 minutes
Makes 6

½ cup old-fashioned rolled oats
1½ cups all-purpose flour
2 teaspoons baking powder
½ teaspoon baking soda
½ cup sugar, plus extra for sprinkling
2 eggs, beaten
6 tablespoons vegetable oil
2 apples, grated

a 6-cup muffin pan, preferably nonstick

Preheat the oven to 350ºF. If necessary, line your muffin pan with paper liners.

Put the oats, flour, baking powder, baking soda, and sugar in a bowl and mix well. Beat together the eggs and oil, and pour into the mixing bowl. Add the grated apple and mix together quickly (overmixing will make the muffins lose their light texture). Spoon the mixture into 6 muffin cases. Sprinkle the top of each with a little extra sugar and bake in the middle of the oven for 30–40 minutes. Test for readiness by inserting a knife: the blade should come out clean. Eat warm or cold.

frozen berry muffins

Spelt is an ancient variety of wheat. Its flour adds texture to these muffins.

Preparation 15 minutes
Cooking 30–40 minutes
Makes 6

1⅔ cups spelt flour
2 teaspoons baking powder
½ teaspoon baking soda
½ cup sugar
2 eggs, beaten
6 tablespoons vegetable oil
1 cup frozen berries (no need to thaw)

a 6-cup muffin pan, preferably nonstick

Preheat the oven to 350ºF. If necessary, line your muffin pan with paper liners.

Put the flour, baking powder, baking soda, and sugar in a bowl and mix well. Beat together the eggs and oil, pour into the mixing bowl, then add the berries. Mix together quickly so that the muffins do not lose their light texture. Spoon into the muffin pan and bake in the middle of the oven for 30–40 minutes. Test for readiness by inserting a knife: the blade should come out clean. Eat warm or cold.

whole wheat banana and chocolate muffins

Preparation 20 minutes
Cooking 40 minutes
Makes 6

1²⁄₃ cups whole wheat flour
2 teaspoons baking powder
½ cup cane sugar
½ cup chocolate chips
2 eggs, beaten
6 tablespoons vegetable oil
2 bananas

a 6-cup muffin pan, preferably nonstick

The chocolate and whole wheat make this a muffin that combines indulgence with virtue. It's also great for using up those overripe bananas in the fruit bowl.

Preheat the oven to 350°F. If necessary, line your muffin pan with paper liners.

Put the flour, baking powder, sugar, and chocolate chips in a bowl and mix well. Beat together the eggs and oil, and pour into the bowl. Mash the bananas with a fork, add to the bowl, and mix together quickly: the mixture will be quite stiff. Take care not to overmix or the muffins will be heavy. Spoon the mixture into the muffin pan and bake in the middle of the oven for 40 minutes. Test for readiness by inserting a knife: the blade should come out clean. Eat warm or cold.

Eggs must surely be one of the most useful and nutritious foods: they're certainly among the most versatile. They are a good source of protein but, unlike many meat and dairy products, they are low in saturated fat and can therefore be eaten up to six times a week. (Only people with a cholesterol problem might want to eat them a bit less.) I always recommend free-range eggs, but make sure you buy from somewhere with a high turnover so that they're really fresh. When you break them open the yolk should have a good dome and the white should be thinner at the edges than around the yolk.

flat eggs

My two little boys always refer to fried eggs as "flat eggs", and this is what we and many of our friends now call them. No matter how you know them, they're a healthy way to start the day.

Cooking 1–2 minutes
Serves 4

3 tablespoons olive oil
4 eggs

Heat the oil in a heavy-based frying pan. When hot, add the eggs, cover the pan, and cook over medium heat for 1 minute. When the egg white is cooked through, lift each egg out with a spatula and serve on toasted whole wheat bread.

boiled eggs

Many of us probably first encountered eggs softly boiled and accompanied by buttered toast "soldiers" for dipping. There's no improving on this classic.

Cooking 4–6 minutes
Serves 4

4 eggs

Boil a kettle of water and pour into a saucepan on the heat. Carefully lower the eggs into the water, then cover and simmer: 4 minutes for soft yolks, 6 minutes for hard. Remove from the pan with a slotted spoon and serve with toast soldiers.

poached eggs

There's no need to be nervous about poaching eggs in a pan of water, but if you prefer, you can use an egg poacher. The shape is not as relaxed, but they taste just the same.

Cooking 6–8 minutes
Serves 4

4 eggs

Boil a kettle of water and pour into a large saucepan. Crack the eggs into 4 cups, stir the water with a spoon, and gently slip each egg into it. Bring to a gentle simmer, then cover with a lid, remove from the heat, and let stand: 5 minutes for soft poached eggs, and slightly longer if you prefer the yolk hard. Lift the eggs from the water with a slotted spoon and rest on a paper towel to remove any excess water. Serve on toast, perhaps with a slice of ham underneath the egg.

omelet

Whether plain or filled with whatever you happen to have in the fridge, omelets are a great standby meal. My boys and I often make a large one and cut it into portions, which means we can all eat at the same time.

Preparation 5 minutes
Cooking 5 minutes
Serves 3

6 eggs
6 tablespoons milk
3 tablespoons butter
sea salt and freshly ground black pepper

Whisk together the eggs, milk, and seasoning. Melt the butter in a large nonstick frying pan, then pour in the egg mixture, using a fork to lift the set egg and let the liquid egg flow underneath. Cook until the top is just soft. Using a narrow spatula, fold over one-third of the omelet, then turn out and fold over again. Cut into portions and serve at the table.

eggs cocotte

These baked eggs go down a treat at breakfast, or as a light meal when time is short.

Preparation 10 minutes
Cooking 6 minutes
Serves 4

2 oz. fresh spinach, chopped
4 eggs
4 tablespoons milk
¾ cup Parmesan cheese, grated
sea salt and freshly ground black pepper

4 ovenproof ramekins, buttered

Preheat the oven to 400°F. Divide the spinach between the prepared ramekins. Crack an egg on top, add a spoonful of milk to each, then season and top with the Parmesan. Place the ramekins on a baking sheet in the preheated oven and cook for 6 minutes.

scrambled eggs

There are two ways of cooking scrambled eggs:
in the microwave or on the stovetop in a nonstick
pan. I prefer the second method because it allows
you to stir the eggs to creamy perfection.

Preparation 2 minutes
Cooking 3 minutes
Serves 2–3

6 eggs
4 tablespoons milk
2 tablespoons butter
sea salt and freshly ground black pepper
chopped chives, to serve

Whisk the eggs together with the milk and seasoning.
Melt the butter in a medium nonstick pan, then add the
egg mixture, stirring frequently until it reaches a creamy
consistency. Serve with a sprinkling of chopped chives
and hot buttered toast. For a real treat add a few slices
of smoked salmon.

family lunch boxes

I am a great fan of packed lunches because I know exactly
what my children are eating. When they get in from school I can
see what's left and we can have a chat about it so that I can try
to give them other healthy alternatives.

Forget soggy sandwiches, limp crackers, and fatty chips. Think
instead of crunchy salads, light ciabatta rolls filled with hummus,
ham, and cucumber, noodles with shredded chicken, pesto and
Parmesan pasta, tortillas, muffins… the possibilities are endless.
When time is short do not be afraid of buying a good-quality
turkey sandwich and putting it in a box with carrot sticks,
cucumber, and a few crisp lettuce leaves. Every so often it's
necessary to compromise—even in my kitchen!

Don't forget that the grown-ups in the family also deserve a
healthy lunch, so invest in some good lunch boxes that do not
leak, and buy small thermoses for colder months, when you can
fill them with hearty soups.

spicy vegetable wrap

Preparation 10 minutes
Serves 4

4 flatbreads
harissa (optional)
2 carrots, grated
1 zucchini, grated
2 scallions, finely chopped
½ cup half-baked tomatoes
8 iceberg lettuce leaves, chopped

The spice in this wrap comes from harissa, a red Moroccan paste (see page 117). If your family doesn't like spicy food, simply leave it out.

Spread the flatbreads with hariss, if using, leaving a 1-inch border around the edge. Sprinkle with a layer of grated carrot, then layers of zucchini, scallions, tomatoes, and lettuce.

Roll the flat bread up tightly into a cigar shape. Cut in half across the middle, then wrap in plastic wrap, and pop in the lunchbox.

ham and cheese flatbread

Preparation 5 minutes
Cooking 10 minutes
Serves 4

8 x 7-inch flatbreads
8 slices prosciutto or very thinly sliced ham
8 slices Gruyère, Emmental, or other hard cheese
sea salt and freshly ground black pepper
olive oil, for frying

This is something like an instant pizza. While great for lunch boxes, it's also good cut into small pieces and served with drinks.

Lay out four of the flatbreads and cover each with 2 slices of ham and 2 slices of cheese. Season and top with the remaining breads.

Heat a frying pan large enough to hold one whole flat-bread sandwich. Brush with a little olive oil and fry for 2–3 minutes on each side, until golden. Repeat with the remaining sandwiches. Cut into wedges and serve hot or cold.

classic smoked salmon bagel

Preparation 10 minutes
Serves 4

4 bagels
3 oz. cream cheese
½ cucumber, sliced
6½ oz. smoked salmon
½ lemon
sea salt and freshly ground black pepper

This is an elegant way of adding fish oils to your diet—and it couldn't be more delicious.

Cut the bagels in half and spread with the cream cheese. Top with some cucumber and slivers of smoked salmon, season, and squeeze a little lemon juice over. Sandwich together and enjoy!

carrot, chicken, and toasted sesame pouch

Preparation 10 minutes
Serves 4

4 pita breads
4 carrots, grated
6½ oz. cooked chicken, cut into thin strips
2 tablespoons sesame seeds, toasted
1 tablespoon sesame oil
sea salt and freshly ground black pepper

Pack tasty ingredients into a pita bread and you have a great transportable meal. The grated carrot makes it lovely and moist.

Toast the pita breads and slit open to cool. Put the carrots in a bowl with the chicken, add the sesame seeds, oil, and seasoning and mix well. Generously fill the pouches and wrap in plastic wrap.

Think of dips and most of us usually think of parties—but they're so light and delicious that they deserve to be eaten on other occasions too. In fact, they're terrific portable food, so they're ideal for lunch boxes. Serve them with a colorful selection of crudités, some breadsticks or crackers and you have a healthy lunch that's high in lots of essential vitamins and minerals.

guacamole

Preparation 15 minutes
Makes about 2 cups

juice of 1 lemon or lime
3 scallions, thinly sliced
3 tomatoes, peeled, seeded and chopped
1 small green or red fresh chile, finely diced
1 garlic clove, finely chopped
2 ripe avocados
a bunch of fresh cilantro, chopped
2 tablespoons olive oil
sea salt and freshly ground black pepper

Although avocados are high in fat, they are also full of other valuable nutrients. The lovely color will entice the most reluctant eater.

Put the lemon juice in a mixing bowl with the scallions, tomatoes, chile, and garlic. Peel and finely dice the avocado, add to the bowl, and mix well. Add the cilantro, olive oil, and seasoning and mix well. Serve with tortilla chips or crunchy vegetable sticks.

harissa and herb dip

Preparation 20 minutes
Cooking 50 minutes
Serves 4–6

1 quantity harissa (see page 117)
a bunch of fresh cilantro, finely chopped
a bunch of fresh flat-leaf parsley, finely chopped

This lovely dip has a warming spiciness that makes it irresistible. Keep a jar of it in the fridge to spice up sandwiches.

Make the harissa as described on page 117. When cool, stir in the cilantro and parsley and serve with baked fish, barbecued chicken, or lamb. It can also be stirred through new potatoes, rice, or chickpeas.

lemony hummus

Preparation 10 minutes
+ overnight soaking
Cooking 1 hour 30 minutes
Serves 4

1 cup dried chickpeas
1 tablespoon tahini
5 tablespoons olive oil
juice of ½ lemon
2 garlic cloves, crushed
sea salt and freshly ground black pepper

The flavor of this hummus is fresh and delicious—so different from the commercial variety that it might take a little time for some family members to be converted. Rest assured, they will come around...

Put the chickpeas in a bowl, cover generously with cold water, and let soak for 12 hours. Drain, transfer to a small saucepan, and cover with fresh water. Bring to a boil and allow to bubble furiously for 10 minutes. Lower the heat and simmer for 1½ hours, until soft. Add more water if needed. Drain and reserve the cooking water.

Put the chickpeas in a food processor. Add the tahini, olive oil, lemon juice, garlic, and about ⅓ cup of the reserved water. Season and blend until smooth and creamy. Adjust the consistency if you wish by adding more of the cooking water. (You cannot overblend this: it just gets better.) Serve with vegetable sticks or warm pita bread to dip.

cheese dip

Preparation 5 minutes
Serves 4

5 oz. soft blue cheese, such as Danablu
2½ oz. cream cheese
1 tablespoon olive oil

This tasty dip is naughty on the hips but simple to make and truly delicious!

Put the two cheeses in a bowl and mash with a fork. Transfer to a serving bowl and drizzle with the olive oil. Serve with crackers, whole wheat toast or vegetable sticks.

tzatziki

Preparation 10 minutes + 45 minutes
for straining
Makes about 2 cups

1 cucumber, grated
a bunch of fresh mint, chopped
2 garlic cloves, crushed
1½ cups Greek yogurt
sea salt and freshly ground black pepper

The clean flavors of this Greek dip make it really refreshing on a summer's day.

Put the cucumber in a strainer over a bowl and leave for 45 minutes, until the excess liquid has dripped out. Mix the remaining ingredients together, then season and add the cucumber. Stir well and serve with toasted pita bread and vegetable sticks.

oven-roasted vegetables with chickpeas and couscous

Preparation 30 minutes
Cooking 40 minutes
Serves 4

2 tablespoons olive oil
2 garlic cloves, chopped
1 teaspoon sweet paprika
2 red onions, cut into wedges
1 large red pepper, seeded and sliced
1 small butternut squash, unpeeled, cut into wedges
6½ oz. cherry or grape tomatoes
3 oz. green beans, trimmed
2 sprigs of fresh thyme
1¼ cups couscous
1 cup cooked chickpeas, drained
juice and finely grated zest of 1 unwaxed lemon
sea salt and freshly ground black pepper

Give vegetables a new lease of life by roasting them until they are deliciously caramelized and serving them with couscous.

Preheat the oven to 400°F. Lightly oil a large roasting pan.

Pour the olive oil into a large bowl and add the garlic and paprika. Season well and mix. Place the prepared vegetables in the bowl along with the tomatoes and green beans. Stir until they are well coated with the flavored oil.

Put the vegetables in the prepared roasting pan with the sprigs of thyme. Cook in the oven for 20 minutes, moving them around at intervals (using a large metal spoon) to ensure even roasting. Reduce the heat to 350°F and roast for a further 20 minutes.

Put the couscous in a large bowl and add 1¼ cups hot water, stir well, cover, and let stand for 5–10 minutes. Meanwhile, put the chickpeas in a saucepan of boiling water and allow them to boil for 2 minutes. Drain and add the chickpeas to the couscous, mixing well to fluff up the grains. Add the roasted vegetables.

Put 4 tablespoons hot water into the roasting pan and mix well to combine with the vegetable juices. Spoon this mixture over the vegetables and couscous. Add the lemon juice and zest and fold everything together. Spoon individual portions into airtight containers and store in the fridge until needed.

lentil and baked tomato salad

Preparation 10 minutes
Cooking 50 minutes
Serves 4

2 cups dried green "Puy" lentils
8 oz. cherry tomatoes
½ cup pitted olives
2½ oz. Parmesan cheese
2 tablespoons balsamic vinegar
sea salt and freshly ground black pepper
olive oil, for baking and dressing

Green French lentils are a must for this recipe as they do not collapse when cooked. They give this salad fantastic flavor and texture.

Put the lentils in a saucepan, cover with water, and bring to a boil. Lower the heat and simmer for 40 minutes, until soft.

Preheat the oven to 250°F. Put the tomatoes on a nonstick baking sheet, drizzle 3 tabespoons of olive oil over them, then put in the oven and bake for 40 minutes.

Drain the lentils when cooked and place in a serving bowl. Add the tomatoes, olives, and seasoning. Grate the Parmesan over the top and drizzle with olive oil and balsamic vinegar. Lightly mix and serve.

kidney bean, egg, and ham salad

Preparation 20 minutes
+ overnight soaking
Cooking 1 hour 40 minutes
Serves 4

1 cup dried kidney beans
2 heads Boston or butterhead lettuce
6½ oz. cooked ham, chopped
4 hard-boiled eggs, quartered
a bunch of fresh parsley, chopped
Dressing
1 teaspoon Dijon mustard
1 teaspoon honey
1 tablespoon red wine vinegar
1 garlic clove, crushed
½ teaspoon sugar
3 tablespoons olive oil
sea salt and freshly ground black pepper

The joy of this salad is that it contains a generous amount of essential nutrients—and it tastes great!

Soak the beans in a large bowl of water overnight. Drain and transfer to a saucepan, cover with water and bring to a boil. Allow to bubble furiously for 10 minutes, then simmer for 1 hour 20 minutes, until soft. Add more water while cooking, if needed, then drain, rinse, and cool.

Separate the lettuce leaves and use to line a salad bowl. Add the kidney beans, ham, and eggs. Whisk together the dressing ingredients, then pour over the salad and sprinkle with the parsley. Toss before serving.

thai chicken noodle salad

Most people love noodles, and the delicate spiciness in this recipe should not overpower sensitive taste buds. However, you can seed the chiles if you prefer a milder flavor.

Preparation 20 minutes
Cooking 10 minutes
Serves 4

1 tablespoon vegetable oil
12 oz. chicken breast, thinly sliced
½ inch fresh ginger, peeled and chopped
2 garlic cloves, crushed
1 lemongrass stick, thinly sliced
1 medium-hot fresh chile, finely diced
10 oz. thick noodles
3 oz. bok choy, chopped
1 lime, to serve

Heat the oil in a wok or large frying pan, add the chicken, ginger, garlic, lemongrass, and chile, stir well and cook over medium heat for 5 minutes.

Meanwhile, cook the noodles according to the package instructions, then drain.

Add the bok choy and cooked noodles to the wok and toss well. Serve with lime wedges.

ginger vegetable noodles

Even reluctant vegetable eaters will enjoy this. Its glorious colors are hard to resist.

Preparation 20 minutes
Cooking 10 minutes
Serves 4

10 oz. noodles
2 tablespoons sesame oil
2 inches fresh ginger, peeled and chopped
2 garlic cloves, crushed
2 teaspoons miso
3½ oz. green beans, trimmed
3½ oz. snow peas, trimmed
3½ oz. small asparagus, trimmed
3½ oz. baby sweet corn
2 cups fresh bean sprouts
1 tablespoon soy sauce
1 teaspoon sugar
a bunch of fresh cilantro, chopped
4 scallions, thinly sliced

Cook the noodles according to the package instructions. Drain and toss in 1 tablespoon of sesame oil to stop them sticking together. Set aside.

Heat a tablespoon of oil in a wok or large frying pan, add the ginger and garlic and cook briefly without browning. Add the miso and ½ cup water and simmer for 5 minutes. Stir in the green beans, snow peas, asparagus, and corn and cook for 2 minutes. Add the bean sprouts, soy sauce, sugar, and noodles, toss well, then transfer to a thermos. Put the cilantro and scallions in a small pot to add just before eating.

rice noodle salad with shrimp

A delicious and sustaining lunch. If you'd like to spice it up a little more for adults, add some chopped scallions, fresh cilantro, and red chile.

Preparation 15 minutes
Cooking 10 minutes
Serves 6

5 oz. thin rice noodles
2 tablespoons vegetable oil
½ inch fresh ginger, peeled and chopped
1 garlic clove, chopped
6 oz. cooked peeled shrimp
2 oz. fine green beans, trimmed
1 carrot, cut into matchsticks
juice of ½ a lime
¼ cup chopped cashew nuts
1 tablespoon sesame seeds, toasted

Cook the noodles according to the package instructions. Drain, toss them in a little of the oil, and let cool in the colander for 10 minutes.

Heat the remaining oil in a wok or large frying pan and add the ginger, garlic, shrimp, beans, and carrot. Cook over medium heat for 4 minutes, stirring constantly. Add the mixture to the cooled noodles and mix well. Spoon individual portions into airtight containers and top with a sprinkling of cashew nuts and toasted sesame seeds.

parmesan and ham straws

Cheese straws are great "mobile food." Serve them in lunch boxes or at drinks parties.

Preparation 30 minutes
Cooking 30 minutes
Makes 12-15

1 lb. frozen puff pastry dough, thawed

1 egg, beaten

6½ oz. Parmesan or other hard cheese, grated

4 slices prosciutto

Preheat the oven to 350°F.

Dust a work surface with flour and unfold the pastry dough. Brush all over with half of the beaten egg. Cut the pastry in half and sprinkle one half with all but ½ cup of the cheese. Cover with the prosciutto and place the remaining pastry on top. Roll firmly together. Cut into strips 1 inch wide and 6 inches long, then carefully twist each one about 2 or 3 times.

Place the straws on a baking sheet, brush with the remaining egg, and sprinkle with the remaining cheese. Bake for 30 minutes, until puffed and golden.

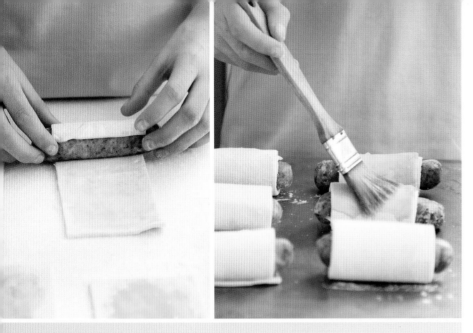

sausage rolls

Ideal for lunch boxes and picnics. Use good-quality sausages for these top-notch rolls.

Preparation 20 minutes
Cooking 45 minutes
Makes 6

1 lb. frozen puff pastry dough, thawed
1 egg, beaten
6 sausages
flour, for dusting

Preheat the oven to 350°F.

Dust a work surface with flour and unfold the pastry. Cut the pastry into three strips just smaller in width than the sausages. Brush all over with beaten egg. Place a sausage at the end of one strip and roll up, using half the strip. Cut the pastry, pat it firmly around the sausage, then place seam-side down on a baking sheet. Repeat this process with the remaining sausages.

Brush each roll with beaten egg and make a few small slashes in the top with a sharp knife. Place in the middle of the oven and bake for 30 minutes. Reduce the heat to 300°F and cook for a further 15 minutes. Serve hot or cold.

chorizo and bean pasties

If you've never had chorizo, you're in for a treat. It's a Spanish sausage, available in various degrees of spiciness, and is just delicious.

Preparation 30 minutes
Cooking 40 minutes
Makes 4

1¼ cups white beans, cooked and drained
5 oz. chorizo, chopped
2 oz. Manchego or other hard cheese, grated
flour, for dusting
1 lb. frozen puff pastry dough, thawed
1 egg, beaten
sea salt and freshly ground black pepper

Preheat the oven to 350°F. Lightly oil a baking sheet.

Put the white beans in a bowl, add the chorizo, cheese, and flour, season and mix well. Pour in ¼ cup water and stir again.

Lightly dust a work surface with flour and unfold the pastry dough. Cut into 4 equal squares and spoon the chorizo mixture into the middle of each one. Brush the edges with beaten egg, then fold two opposite corners together to make a triangular shape. Press all around the edges to seal.

Place the pasties on a baking sheet and brush the tops with beaten egg. Make a small slash in the top of each pasty, then bake in the middle of the oven for 40 minutes. These can be eaten hot or cold.

chicken soup

Preparation 20 minutes
Cooking 40 minutes
Serves 4

1 tablespoon olive oil
1 onion, chopped
1 garlic clove, crushed
2 boneless, skinless chicken breasts, diced
2 leeks, chopped
2 medium potatoes, unpeeled and chopped
6 cups chicken stock
3 sprigs of thyme
2 bay leaves
kernels from 1 cob of sweet corn (about 1 cup)
sea salt and freshly ground black pepper

A bowlful of this comforting soup makes everyone feel better, especially when served with warm homemade bread (see page 25).

Heat the olive oil in a saucepan, add the onion, garlic, chicken, and leeks and sauté gently for 8 minutes without browning. Add the potatoes, stock, thyme, and bay leaves, then season and simmer for 20 minutes.

Add the corn to the soup and cook for a further 10 minutes. Remove the thyme and bay leaves before serving.

pea and ham soup

Preparation 15 minutes
Cooking 40 minutes
Serves 4

2 tablespoons olive oil
1 onion, chopped
8 oz. cooked ham, chopped
6 cups vegetable or ham stock
2 cups fresh or frozen peas, (no need to thaw)
sea salt and freshly ground black pepper

Easy to make and hearty enough for the coldest winter's day. People of all ages love this soup.

Heat the oil in a saucepan, add the onion, and sauté for 5 minutes without browning. Add the ham, then pour in the stock, and bring to a boil. Lower the heat and simmer for 25 minutes.

Add the peas, and some seasoning, and cook for a further 5 minutes. (Frozen peas should be cooked for a little longer.) Transfer the soup to a blender or food processor, and blitz until smooth. Adjust the consistency if you wish by adding a little more stock or water, and serve topped with a drizzle of olive oil.

quick weekday suppers

Busy days spent working or dashing around after the children can leave you weary and dreading the thought of preparing the evening meal. This needn't be the case if you ensure you always have a stock of basic ingredients and you have some easy recipes up your sleeve that you feel confident about cooking. The ideas in the following pages all fit that bill.

In many families eating together has become something of a lost tradition, or it's done in front of the television, and I think that's a real pity. Mealtimes are a great opportunity for relaxing and sharing news and ideas: they really do bring the family closer together. If you and yours have lost the habit of sitting round the dinner table, try to make it a rule that you all eat together at least once a week. On days when you all have different commitments and it's just not possible, make a dish that lends itself to being kept warm or reheated so that people can help themselves as they come and go. Ideal dishes include Italian meatballs, three-cheese cauliflower, Lancashire hotpot, and easy tuna patties, all served with mashed potatoes (which won't spoil).

chicken and broccoli noodles

Preparation 10 minutes
Cooking 15 minutes
Serves 4

10 oz. egg noodles
1 tablespoon vegetable oil
3 boneless, skinless chicken breasts, cut into strips
1½ cups broccoli florets
1 garlic clove, crushed
1 red chile, diced (optional)
⅓ cup sesame seeds, toasted
½ cup cashew nuts
1 tablespoon sesame oil
soy sauce, to serve

Tasty, satisfying, and healthy—what more could you want from a quick weekday supper?

Cook the noodles according to the package instructions, then drain and set aside.

Heat the oil in a large pan, add the chicken and cook over high heat for 5 minutes, until golden. Stir in the broccoli and cook for 2 minutes. Add the garlic, chile, and sesame seeds and cook for 2 more minutes. Add the noodles, toss well, and cook for a further 3 minutes. Finally, add the cashews and sesame oil, stir through the mixture and serve with soy sauce at the table.

pasta with ham and peas

Preparation 10 minutes
Cooking 10 minutes
Serves 4

10 oz. pasta
1 tablespoon olive oil
1 shallot, diced
1 garlic clove, crushed
6½ oz. cooked ham, chopped
1 cup fresh or frozen peas (no need to thaw)
6 tablespoons heavy cream
2 egg yolks
1 cup freshly grated Parmesan cheese
sea salt and freshly ground black pepper

This classic Italian recipe gives a new twist to ham and eggs.

Bring a large pan of salted water to a boil, add the pasta, and cook according to the package instructions. Drain and return it to the pan.

Meanwhile, heat the oil in a saucepan, add the shallot and garlic, and sauté over low heat until soft.

Put the ham, peas, and cream in another pan and heat to a gentle simmer. Remove from the heat and add the egg yolks, Parmesan, and seasoning. Mix well so that the egg does not scramble. Finally, add the sautéd garlic and shallot, toss through the pasta and serve.

italian meatballs with pasta

Preparation 30 minutes
Cooking 1 hour
Serves 4

4 tablespoons olive oil
2 onions, finely chopped
2 garlic cloves, finely chopped
1 x 28-oz. can chopped tomatoes
½ cup red wine
1 bay leaf and 2 sprigs of thyme
8 oz. ground pork
8 oz. ground beef
a bunch of fresh flat-leaf parsley, chopped
1 egg
10 oz. spaghetti
sea salt and freshly ground black pepper
freshly grated Parmesan cheese, to serve

Offer this with a bowl of dried red pepper flakes so that people can spice it up if they like.

Heat half the oil in a frying pan, add half the onion and garlic, and sauté gently for 5 minutes. Add the tomatoes, wine, bay leaf, thyme, and seasoning, and simmer gently for 30 minutes.

Put the remaining onion and garlic in a large bowl, add the pork, beef, parsley, egg, and seasoning and combine thoroughly. Divide into 16 equal pieces and shape into balls. Heat the remaining oil in a large pan and brown the meatballs all over. Pour the sauce into the pan, then cover and simmer for 20 minutes.

Meanwhile, cook the spaghetti according to the package instructions. Serve topped with the meatballs and grated Parmesan cheese.

sausage and bacon toad-in-the-hole

Preparation 20 minutes
+ 30 minutes resting

Cooking 35 minutes

Serves 4–6

1½ cups flour

2 eggs

⅔ cup milk

8 slices bacon

2 lb. sausages

2 red onions, cut into wedges

sea salt and freshly ground black pepper

A fun Friday night supper that everyone enjoys—especially with a crisp green salad.

Put the flour in a mixing bowl and make a well in the center. Whisk the eggs, milk, and water together and pour into the well. Stir carefully with a wooden spoon until you have a smooth batter. Let rest for 30 minutes.

Preheat the oven to 425°F. Grease a large roasting pan or 4–6 individual dishes and place in the oven.

Wrap the bacon around the sausages and place in the hot roasting pan or dishes. Add the onion, then pour in the batter. Return to the oven and bake for 30 minutes without opening the door. The batter should be light and well risen.

three-cheese cauliflower

Preparation 15 minutes

Cooking 30 minutes

Serves 4

1 cauliflower

3½ oz. Gruyère cheese, grated

3½ oz. Emmental cheese, grated

3½ oz. Beaufort or other hard, strong cheese, grated

1 teaspoon cornstarch

sea salt and freshly ground black pepper

a shallow, 8 x 10 inch ovenproof dish

How can you improve on classic comfort food? In this case, use a variety of cheeses to make it even richer.

Preheat the oven to 375°F.

Cut the cauliflower into florets and plunge them into boiling water. Bring back to the boil, then simmer for 4 minutes and drain well.

Put the cheeses in a bowl, sprinkle in the cornstarch, and mix to coat the cheese evenly. Transfer to a nonstick saucepan, add ¾ cup water, and gently bring to a slight simmer, stirring constantly until you have a smooth sauce.

Place the cauliflower in the ovenproof dish and pour the cheese sauce all over it. Bake in the oven for 15 minutes, until golden on top. Take care when serving as the cheese gets extremely hot.

lancashire hotpot

Preparation 15 minutes
Cooking 2 hours 15 minutes
Serves 4–6

2 tablespoons olive oil
2 lb. lamb stewing meat, cut into 2-inch pieces
1 onion, finely diced
2 carrots, finely diced
4 celery ribs, finely diced
2 leeks, thinly sliced
2 tablespoons flour
1 tablespoon Worcestershire sauce
2 lb. potatoes, unpeeled
sea salt and freshly ground black pepper

Inspired by thrift, this dish has transcended its humble origins and become a firm favorite around the world. The golden potato topping hides tender lamb in heavenly gravy.

Heat the olive oil in a large, flameproof casserole dish, add the lamb, and brown all over. Transfer to a plate. Reduce the heat under the casserole, add all the vegetables, and sauté for 10 minutes, stirring frequently.

Remove the casserole from the heat, add the meat, then sprinkle in the flour and mix well. Pour in just enough hot water to cover the meat and vegetables, stir well, and return to the heat.

Preheat the oven to 350°F.

Bring the casserole to a boil, stirring frequently as the gravy thickens. Season and add the Worcestershire sauce. Remove from the heat.

Slice the potatoes thinly by hand or with a mandolin. Layer them carefully over the meat and vegetables, covering them completely. Place in the oven and cook for 2 hours. The potatoes should be golden on top and the gravy bubbling up around the sides.

easy tuna patties

Preparation 15 minutes
Cooking 40 minutes
Serves 4

20 oz. sweet potatoes, peeled
and chopped
10 oz. tuna, flaked
2 scallions, chopped
1 egg
¾ cup cornmeal
3 tablespoons olive oil
sea salt and freshly ground black pepper
1 lemon, to serve

Cornmeal makes a lovely crumb coating on these fish cakes. If using canned tuna, buy a good-quality brand that has a dense texture and large chunks. Alternatively, pan-cook fresh tuna and flake it yourself.

Cook the sweet potatoes in a pan of simmering water for 20 minutes. Drain well and mash. Add the tuna, scallions, and egg, season and mix well. Divide the mixture into 8 equal pieces and shape into patties.

Put the cornmeal on a plate and dip the patties in it until coated on all sides.

Heat the oil and fry the patties on each side until golden. Serve with lemon wedges and a tomato salad.

prosciutto-wrapped salmon on mash

Preparation 15 minutes
Cooking 25 minutes
Serves 4

2 lb. potatoes, unpeeled and diced
1 egg
3 tablespoons butter
4 salmon fillets, about 4 oz. each,
skinned and boned
4 slices prosciutto
a bunch of fresh dill, chopped
sea salt and freshly ground black pepper

Fish such as salmon are rich in omega-3 oils, which are essential for a healthy heart, so here's a recipe that will do your family some extra good!

Preheat the oven to 350°F. Lightly oil a baking sheet.

Bring the potatoes to a boil in a pan of water, then simmer for 20 minutes, until soft. Drain and return to the pan, place over the heat and shake to remove any excess moisture. Mash well, then mix in the egg and seasoning. Add the butter and mash again until creamy.

Meanwhile, season the salmon fillets and wrap in the prosciutto. Place on the prepared baking sheet and cook in the oven for 15 minutes. Sprinkle with the dill and serve with mashed potatoes.

mushroom frittata

Preparation 15 minutes
Cooking 20 minutes
Serves 4–6

1½ tablespoons butter
2 tablespoons olive oil
3 cooked potatoes, diced
6½ oz. flat mushrooms
1 garlic clove, crushed
4 oz. baby spinach
4 eggs
⅓ cup milk
sea salt and freshly ground black pepper

Mushrooms can be an acquired taste among younger members of the family, but this will tempt them to try.

Heat the butter and olive oil in an ovenproof frying pan, add the potatoes, and brown on all sides. Transfer to a plate, then cook the mushrooms on both sides for 5 minutes, adding a little more oil or butter if necesary. Transfer to another plate and return the potatoes to the pan. Sprinkle in the garlic, then add the mushrooms and spinach.

Mix the eggs and milk together, then season and pour into the pan. Cover and cook gently for 5 minutes.

Heat the broiler to medium-high, place the pan under it, and broil for 6–8 minutes, or until golden on top. Check that the egg is set, then serve hot or cold.

green bean risotto

Preparation 15 minutes
Cooking 30 minutes
Serves 4

1 quart chicken or vegetable stock
1 tablespoon olive oil
1 onion, finely chopped
1 garlic clove, crushed
1½ cups arborio rice
3½ oz. green beans, cut into 1-inch pieces
3½ oz. fresh or frozen peas
(no need to thaw)
3½ oz. asparagus, cut into 1-inch pieces
3½ oz. spinach, chopped
1¼ cups freshly grated Parmesan cheese
sea salt and freshly ground black pepper

"Lip-smacking" is how my children describe this creamy risotto. The vegetables can be varied according to what you like and what's in season.

Put the stock in a saucepan and bring to a simmer.

Heat the olive oil in a shallow saucepan and sauté the onions and garlic on a low heat for 5 minutes without browning. Add the rice and stir well to coat in the oil. Add a ladleful of hot stock, stir, and simmer until absorbed. Repeat until almost all the stock has been added.

Add all the vegetables with the last ladleful of stock, mix well, and cook for 2 minutes. The rice should be *al dente*. Stir in half the Parmesan and add some seasoning. When ready to serve, offer the remaining Parmesan separately, plus a little extra olive oil for drizzling if you wish.

get-ahead weekends

Weekends are precious, so if you can get some of the meals planned and prepared in advance, it will give you more time to get out and about with the family, play sports, see friends, ferry the kids to parties, or just enjoy life at home. This section offers lots of ideas to help you do just this.

When cooking during the week, I often try to get ahead by making something for the weekend too. Soups, for example, can be refrigerated or frozen and make a good lunch with fresh bread, a chunk of cheese, and some fruit. Casseroles, curries, and bakes are also good, as they reheat well, and marinated meats can be pan-fried or grilled in a matter of minutes.

On wet weekends my children are often very happy to test their skills in the kitchen, especially if pizzas are on the menu. We all add our own favorite toppings, and what might otherwise be a chore becomes fun. Why not try this with your family?

golden butternut squash soup

Preparation 20 minutes
Cooking 40 minutes
Serves 4

1½ lb. peeled and diced butternut squash
2 tablespoons olive oil
2 onions, diced
1 garlic clove, crushed
6 cups chicken or vegetable stock
sea salt and freshly ground black pepper
light cream, to serve (optional)

Squash is a wonderfully versatile vegetable, and it's used to great effect in this flavorsome soup.

Heat the oil in a large saucepan, add the squash, onions, and garlic and sauté over low heat for 10 minutes. Add the stock, bring to a boil, then simmer for 30 minutes.

Using a hand-held blender, blitz the soup until smooth and creamy. Season and serve with a drizzle of cream, if liked.

sausage and bean soup

Preparation 15 minutes
Cooking 35 minutes
Serves 4

2 tablespoons olive oil
1 onion, diced
2 garlic cloves, crushed
2 carrots, diced
2 celery ribs, diced
6 cups vegetable, ham or chicken stock
1 cup cooked butter beans
1 bay leaf
a sprig of thyme
12 oz. Toulouse or other fresh pork sausage
a handful of fresh parsley, chopped
sea salt and freshly ground black pepper

Toulouse sausage, made from pork, is the key ingredient in this recipe, so do try to get hold of some. Its coarse texture lends itself to this tasty, peasant-style soup.

Heat the oil in a saucepan, add the onion, garlic, carrots, and celery and sauté on a low heat for 10 minutes, until soft. Add the stock, beans, bay leaf, thyme, and sausages, then season and simmer for 25 minutes.

Discard the bay leaf and thyme, then remove the sausages from the pan and slice them. Return to the pan, add the parsley, and stir well.

onion soup

Preparation 20 minutes
Cooking 1 hour 15 minutes
Serves 4

1 tablespoon olive oil
2 tablespoons butter
1½ lb. onions, thinly sliced
2 garlic cloves, crushed
2 tablespoons flour
1 quart beef or vegetable stock
¾ cup red wine
1 bay leaf and a sprig of thyme
a bunch of fresh parsley, finely chopped
4 slices French bread
1 cup grated Gruyère cheese
sea salt and freshly ground black pepper

A traditional French soup that never fails to please. It's always a meal in itself.

Heat the oil and butter in a medium pan, add the onions and garlic, and sauté over low heat for 25 minutes, stirring frequently. The onions should become golden brown and soft.

Sprinkle in the flour and stir to absorb the excess oil. Slowly pour in the stock and wine, mix well, and bring to a gentle simmer. Add the bay leaf, thyme, and seasoning. Cover and simmer for 40 minutes over low heat.

Just before serving, toast the bread under the broiler, top with the grated cheese, and broil until melted. Stir the parsley into the soup, ladle it into bowls, and top with the cheesy toasts.

minestrone with pesto

Preparation 15 minutes
+ overnight soaking
Cooking 2 hours 15 minutes
Serves 4

1 cup dried white beans
1 tablespoon olive oil
1 red onion, chopped
2 garlic cloves, crushed
2 leeks, 2 carrots, and 2 celery ribs, diced
6 cups chicken or vegetable stock
4 thick slices bacon, diced
1½ tablespoons tomato concentrate
1 bay leaf and a small bunch of fresh thyme
½ cup tiny pasta
Pesto
½ cup pine nuts
a generous bunch of fresh basil
2½ oz. Parmesan cheese, grated
2 garlic cloves, crushed
6 tablespoons olive oil

Everyone loves classic minestrone, but for a change you could add some cooked ham or dried chiles. You could also use canned white beans instead of dried.

Cover the beans in cold water and soak overnight. Drain, cover with fresh water, and bring to a boil. Bubble hard for 10 minutes, then simmer for 1½ hours. Drain and set aside.

Heat the oil in a saucepan, add the onion, garlic, leeks, carrots, celery, and lardons, and sauté for 10 minutes over medium heat without browning. Add the beans, stock, tomato concentrate, and herbs, bring to a boil and simmer for 25 minutes.

Meanwhile, make the pesto. Put all the ingredients in a blender or food processor and whiz until smooth. Transfer to a jar, cover with olive oil, and store in the fridge until needed.

When the soup has finished its first simmering, add the pasta and simmer again for 8 minutes, stirring frequently. Season and serve with a spoonful of pesto and lots of crusty bread.

lamb and potato pie

Preparation 25 minutes
Cooking 1 hour 15 minutes
Serves 6

1 tablespoon olive oil
1 onion, diced
2 garlic cloves, crushed
1 celery rib, diced
1 carrot, diced
1½ lb. ground lamb
2 tablespoons flour
1¼ cups stock
1 tablespoon Worcestershire sauce
2 lb. potatoes
2 tablespoons butter
3 tablespoons milk
1 egg
sea salt and freshly ground black pepper
grated cheese, for sprinkling (optional)

You can use beef instead of lamb in this pie, or even half and half. Grated cheese makes a lovely topping.

Preheat the oven to 350°F.

Heat the oil in a large, flameproof casserole, add the onion, garlic, celery, and carrot, and sauté over low heat for 10 minutes. Add the lamb and cook for 5 minutes, breaking up the meat with a wooden spoon. Sprinkle in the flour, mix well, then add the stock, Worcestershire sauce, and seasoning. Stir well, then cover and set aside.

Cook the potatoes in a large pan of boiling water for 20 minutes, drain well, return to the pan, and shake over low heat to steam off any excess moisture. Remove from the heat and mash until smooth. Add the butter, milk, egg, and seasoning, and beat well. Spoon the potatoes over the lamb in the casserole and spread evenly with a fork. Sprinkle with grated cheese, if liked. Bake in the oven for 40 minutes.

macaroni, spinach, and cheese bake

Preparation 10 minutes
Cooking 40 minutes
Serves 4

8 oz. macaroni
3 tablespoons butter
⅓ cup flour
2 cups milk
5 oz. cooked spinach, well drained
3 cups freshly grated Parmesan cheese
sea salt and freshly ground black pepper

a large, ovenproof baking dish

Fresh or frozen spinach can be used in this recipe, but do make sure that both are thoroughly drained.

Cook the macaroni according to the package instructions. Preheat the oven to 375°F.

Meanwhile, melt the butter in a saucepan, remove from the heat, and mix in the flour to make a roux. Return to low heat and slowly pour in the milk, stirring constantly. Bring to a boil and cook for 1 minute, stirring frequently.

Drain the macaroni and add to the sauce along with the spinach, seasoning, and half the cheese. Mix well. Pour the mixture into the ovenproof baking dish, scatter the remaining cheese on top, and bake for 15 minutes, until golden.

beef and carrot casserole with cheesy dumplings

Preparation 30 minutes
Cooking 2 hours
Serves 4–6

1 tablespoon olive oil
2 garlic cloves, crushed
1 onion, diced
2 celery ribs, diced
2 lb. chuck steak, cut into cubes
1²/₃ cups beef stock
¾ cup red wine
2 bay leaves
4 carrots, cut into chunks
2 tablespoons flour
sea salt and freshly ground black pepper

Dumplings
1½ cups flour
⅓ cup shortening
1 teaspoon baking powder
½ cup grated sharp Cheddar cheese

Think of chilly, dark evenings and this is exactly what you'd want to eat. The feather-light dumplings nestling in the rich, savory casserole will have everyone demanding more.

Heat the oil in a large, flameproof casserole, add the garlic, onion, and celery, and sauté for 4 minutes. Transfer to a plate. Put the beef in the casserole, increase the heat, and sauté for 5 minutes, stirring frequently. When the beef is cooked, return the onion mixture to the casserole. Add the stock, red wine, seasoning, and bay leaves, bring to a boil, then reduce the heat to a gentle simmer. Cover and cook for 1½ hours.

To make the dumplings, place the flour and baking powder in a bowl and rub in the shortening until it resembles breadcrumbs. Add the cheese, mixing it in with a knife. Add ¼–⅓ cup cold water and use your hands to bring the mixture together and form a dough. Divide into 8 equal pieces and roll into balls.

Remove the casserole from the heat for 5 minutes, then sift in the flour and stir to thicken the gravy. Return to the heat, add the carrots, and stir until the casserole comes to a simmer. Place the dumplings on top, cover, and cook for 20 minutes.

spaghetti bolognese

Preparation 20 minutes
Cooking 1 hour 15 minutes
Serves 4–6

2 tablespoons olive oil
3 garlic cloves, crushed
2 onions, diced
1 celery rib, diced
1 carrot, diced
1¾ lb. ground beef
a bunch of fresh oregano, chopped
a sprig of thyme
2 bay leaves
3 x 14-oz. cans chopped tomatoes
10 oz. spaghetti
a handful of fresh parsley, chopped
sea salt and freshly ground black pepper
freshly grated Parmesan cheese, to serve

Long, slow cooking is the secret of good Bolognese sauce. It can be served with any shape of pasta, and a crisp green salad is the perfect accompaniment.

Heat the oil in a large saucepan, add the garlic, onions, celery, and carrot, and sauté gently for 10 minutes. Add the beef, breaking it up with a wooden spoon, and cook for a further 10 minutes. Add the oregano, thyme, bay leaves, and chopped tomatoes, season, and mix well. Simmer for 1 hour, stirring frequently.

Cook the spaghetti according to the package instructions. Drain well and divide between individual plates. Stir the parsley into the sauce, then spoon onto the pasta and serve.

chili con carne

Preparation 20 minutes
Cooking 1 hour 15 minutes
Serves 4–6

1 quantity Bolognese sauce (see above)
1 tablespoon cayenne pepper
1 tablespoon paprika
1 glass of red wine
2 x 15-oz. cans red kidney beans, drained and rinsed
a handful of cilantro, chopped

Simple dishes are often the best, and they don't come much simpler than this. You can add more or less cayenne pepper, depending on how spicy you like your food.

Make the Bolognese sauce as described above, but also add the cayenne, paprika, wine, and beans listed here before simmering for 1 hour.

Just before serving, stir in the cilantro and serve with bread or boiled rice and a bowl of guacamole (see page 39).

traditional fish cakes

Preparation 40 minutes
Cooking 40 minutes
Serves 4

2 lb. potatoes, peeled
3 tablespoons butter
¼ cup milk
1 lb. salmon, cod, or halibut, skinned
3 eggs
a bunch of fresh parsley, chopped
¾ cup flour, plus extra for dusting
2 cups breadcrumbs
1¼ cups olive oil
sea salt and freshly ground black pepper

These fish cakes freeze well, so are useful for get-ahead weekends. Any type of fish can be used.

Cook the potatoes in boiling water for 20 minutes, Drain, return to the pan, and shake over low heat to dry off. Mash the potatoes, add the butter and milk, and mix well.

Preheat the oven to 350°F. Lightly oil a shallow ovenproof dish. Put the fish into the prepared dish, cover with foil, and bake for 10 minutes. Set aside to cool, then flake the fish into the potato. Beat one egg and add to the mixture, followed by the parsley and seasoning. Mix well.

Put the flour, breadcrumbs, and remaining eggs in 3 separate bowls. Whisk the eggs. Divide the fish mixture into 8 equal pieces and shape into patties. Dust each fish cake with flour, then use one hand to dip them into the egg; use the other hand to coat in the breadcrumbs. Try to get an even coating.

Heat the oil and fry the fish cakes on each side for 5 minutes, until golden. Serve with hollandaise sauce (see page 116).

vegetable, seed, and nut cakes

Preparation 40 minutes
Cooking 40 minutes
Serves 4

2½ cups mashed potato
1 cup cooked spinach
1¼ cups olive oil
3½ oz. mushrooms, chopped
1 garlic clove, crushed
1 zucchini, grated
¾ cup pumpkin seeds
⅓ cup sesame seeds
¾ cup peanuts, chopped
sea salt and freshly ground black pepper

A delicious alternative to fish patties, especially if you have vegetarians in the family, but even non-veggies will happily tuck into these.

Mix the mashed potatoes with the spinach in a bowl. Heat 1 tablespoon of the oil in a frying pan, gently sauté the mushrooms and garlic for 5 minutes, then add to the potato mixture. Add the zucchini and seasoning and stir well. Divide into 8 equal pieces and roll into balls.

Mix the seeds and nuts together on a large plate and roll the balls in the mixture to coat well. Gently flatten them into patties. Heat the remaining oil in a frying pan and cook the patties on each side until golden, about 3–4 minutes.

thai green chicken curry

Preparation 20 minutes
Cooking 20 minutes
Serves 4

2 tablespoons vegetable oil
1 onion, sliced
2 inches fresh ginger, peeled and sliced
2 garlic cloves, crushed
1 lemongrass stick, chopped
1 mild green chile, diced
4 chicken breast fillets, sliced
2 kaffir lime leaves
2 tablespoons Thai green curry paste
¾ cup coconut milk
juice of 1 lime
½ cup broccoli florets
½ cup green beans, trimmed
sea salt and freshly ground black pepper
a bunch of fresh basil, to serve

There is a wonderful fragrance to Thai curries, and they make a fantastic family meal. Build up the chile content gradually until you find a spiciness that everyone enjoys.

Heat the oil in a large saucepan, add the onion, ginger, garlic, lemongrass, and chile, and cook over low heat for 5 minutes. Add the chicken and cook for a further 5 minutes.

Add the kaffir lime leaves and curry paste and mix well. Shake the can of coconut milk and slowly pour into the curry, mixing constantly. Pour in ⅓ cup water and the lime juice, bring to a simmer, and cook gently for 5 minutes. Add the broccoli and beans and simmer for another 3 minutes. Serve in bowls, topped with torn basil leaves. Plain boiled jasmine rice is a good accompaniment.

indian lamb curry

Preparation 20 minutes
Cooking 1 hour 30 minutes–2 hours
Serves 4–6

2 tablespoons vegetable oil
1 onion, sliced
2 inches fresh ginger, peeled and chopped
1 mild red chile, chopped
3 garlic cloves, crushed
1 teaspoon garam masala
1 teaspoon mild curry powder
2 lb. lamb stewing meat, cut into 1-inch pieces
1 x 14-oz. can chopped tomatoes
a bunch of fresh cilantro, chopped
sea salt and freshly ground black pepper

Get the younger family members to help with all the chopping in this recipe. My boys love the different colors and smells.

Heat half the oil in a large pan, add the onion, ginger, chile, and garlic, and cook over high heat for 1 minute, stirring constantly. Add the spices and cook for a further minute. Transfer to a plate.

Heat the remaining tablespoon of oil in the pan and fry the lamb briskly until browned, about 5 minutes. Return the onion mixture to the pan and add the tomatoes. Season and pour in just enough water to cover. Bring to a boil, then lower the heat, cover, and simmer for 1½–2 hours, stirring occasionally. The lamb should be tender and the sauce thick.

Just before serving, add the cilantro. Serve with basmati rice and a bowl of plain yogurt to calm down the spiciness.

shrimp curry

Preparation 15 minutes
Cooking 15 minutes
Serves 4

2 tablespoons vegetable oil
1 onion, grated
3 garlic cloves, crushed
2 inches fresh ginger, peeled and sliced
1 mild red chile, chopped
1 teaspoon turmeric
2 teaspoons curry powder
1 teaspoon ground coriander
1 teaspoon ground cumin
1 lb. cooked peeled shrimp, defrosted
1 x 14-oz. can chopped tomatoes
juice of 2 limes
a bunch of fresh cilantro, chopped
sea salt and freshly ground black pepper

Tiger or jumbo shrimp are ideal for this colorful, citrus-flavored curry.

Heat the oil in a large pan, add the onion, garlic, ginger, and chile, and cook for 5 minutes over medium heat. Add the turmeric, curry powder, ground coriander, and cumin, and mix well. Add the shrimp and cook for 3 minutes.

Pour in the tomatoes and lime juice, add seasoning, and bring to a boil. Reduce the heat and simmer for 5 minutes. Add the chopped cilantro and serve with basmati rice.

vegetable curry

Preparation 30 minutes
Cooking 30 minutes
Serves 4–8

2 tablespoons vegetable oil
1 red onion, sliced
1 garlic clove, crushed
2 mild chiles (1 red, 1 green), chopped
1 teaspoon curry powder
1 teaspoon ground coriander
$1/2$ teaspoon fenugreek
2 medium potatoes, chopped
10 oz. diced butternut squash
1 eggplant, chopped
1 zucchini, chopped
5 oz. green beans, trimmed
1 cup plain yogurt
a bunch of fresh cilantro, chopped
sea salt and freshly ground black pepper

Indian cuisine has a huge variety of vegetable curries, and this recipe offers one that is simple yet very satisfying—perfect weekend fare.

Heat the oil in a large frying pan, add the onion, garlic, and chiles, and sauté for 5 minutes. Stir in the curry powder, coriander, and fenugreek. Add the potatoes, squash, eggplant, and zucchini, and mix well to cover in the spices. Pour in $1 1/4$ cups water, then cover and simmer for 20 minutes, stirring occasionally. Add more water if needed.

When the vegetables are tender, add the green beans, then season and cook for 5 minutes. Remove from the heat, let cool for 3 minutes, then add the yogurt and cilantro. Mix well and serve with warm naan or other flatbread.

lamb pilaf

Preparation 15 minutes
Cooking 2 hours
Serves 4

3 tablespoons olive oil
1 onion, chopped
2 garlic cloves, crushed
5 cardamom pods, crushed
1 cinnamon stick
3 bay leaves
1/3 cup almonds
1 lb. lamb stewing meat, cut into
1-inch pieces
1/3 cup golden raisins
1/3 cup dried apricots
2 cups basmati rice
a handful of chopped fresh parsley

Pilafs are rice dishes that originated in the Middle East. They can be made with meat, poultry, or seafood, and spiced in a variety of ways.

Heat 1 tablespoon of the oil in a large, flameproof casserole dish, add the onion and garlic, and fry for 5 minutes. Add the cardamom, cinnamon, bay leaves, and almonds, and cook for a further 4 minutes. Transfer to a plate.

Heat the remaining oil and fry the lamb on high heat until browned all over. Return the onion mixture to the pan along with the raisins and apricots. Pour in just enough water to cover, then bring to a boil, cover, and simmer for 1 1/2 hours.

Add the rice, stir well, and cover with water. Bring to a boil, then cover and simmer very gently for 30 minutes. Add the chopped parsley and serve.

spare ribs

Preparation 10 minutes
+ overnight marinating
Cooking 50 minutes
Serves 4

16 pork spare ribs
Marinade
1 tablespoon honey
1 tablespoon dark soy sauce
2 garlic cloves, crushed
zest and juice of 1 unwaxed lemon
1 tablespoon sugar
2 tablespoons tomato concentrate
1 tablespoon Worcestershire sauce
1 teaspoon red wine vinegar
2 teaspoons Dijon mustard
sea salt and freshly ground black pepper

Finger food comes in all shapes and sizes, but none better than these yummy spare ribs—a lovely weekend treat for all the family.

Put all the marinade ingredients in a large bowl and mix until smooth. Add the ribs to the bowl, turn to coat, and let marinate overnight in the refrigerator, turning frequently.

Preheat the oven to 350°F. Lightly oil a roasting pan.

Transfer the ribs to the prepared roasting pan, cover with foil, and bake for 30 minutes. Remove the foil and bake for a further 10 minutes, basting now and again. Turn the ribs and cook for a further 10 minutes, continuing to baste occasionally. Serve with noodles, rice, or salad.

tomato, basil, and mozzarella pizza

Younger family members never seem to tire of pizza, so get them involved in the making as well as the eating.

Preparation 40 minutes + 1–2 hours proving
Cooking 40 minutes
Serves 2

3½ cups all-purpose flour
2 packages rapid-rise yeast
a pinch of salt
a pinch of sugar
1 cup warm water
2 tablespoons olive oil
Topping
4 tablespoons olive oil
1 small onion, finely diced
2 garlic cloves, crushed
1 x 14-oz. can tomato purée
a pinch of dried oregano
8 oz. cherry tomatoes
2 mozzarella balls, sliced
a large bunch of fresh basil
sea salt and freshly ground black pepper

Put the flour, yeast, salt, and sugar in a bowl, make a well in the center, then add the water and oil, and gradually draw in the flour to make a smooth dough. Knead for 12 minutes on a lightly floured work surface. Return the dough to the bowl, drizzle with a little oil, then cover and leave in a warm place until doubled in size. This will take 1–2 hours, depending on the warmth.

To make the topping, heat half the oil in a medium saucepan, add the onion and garlic, and sauté over medium heat for 6 minutes. Add the tomato purée, oregano, and the remaining oil, season and bring to a simmer. Cook for 25 minutes, stirring frequently. The sauce should be thick and full of flavor.

Preheat the oven to 375°F. Lightly oil 2 baking sheets. Knock the air out of the dough and knead for 5 minutes. Cut the dough in half, roll each piece into a ball, and let rest for 10 minutes. Lightly flour a work surface and flatten each piece of dough into a circle about 10 inches in diameter. Place each on a prepared baking sheet and add the tomato mixture, spreading it with the back of a spoon. Top with the cherry tomatoes and sliced mozzarella, season, and drizzle with a little extra olive oil. Put in the oven and bake for 12–15 minutes. Scatter with torn basil leaves, then cut into wedges and serve.

sunday dinner

There's no doubt that Sunday dinner is the highlight of the week in many families—even in these days of fast food. Everyone loves a succulent roast with all the trimmings, and every family has its own special recipes and traditions associated with it. Some have mint sauce with lamb, others prefer red currant jelly. (I serve both.) Some have Yorkshire pudding with roast beef; others have it with everything. Whatever your preferences, I think it's essential to make real gravy, using the juices from the roasting pan. Nothing out of a package or jar tastes as good.

Of course, Sunday dinner does not have to be a roast: it can be anything you like—perhaps a homemade egg and bacon tart or a large dish of lasagne. Whatever you make, don't forget to serve vegetables. Choose the best of what's in season and prepare them a little differently to tempt everyone to have some. Spiced red cabbage, roast sesame carrots, and cauliflower in cheese sauce are just a few of the possibilities. Make your Sunday dinner a tradition that no one will want to miss.

roast chicken with lemon, thyme, and potato stuffing

Preparation 20 minutes

Cooking approx. 1 hour 20 minutes

Serves 4

1 medium free-range chicken

1 unwaxed lemon, thinly sliced

4 bay leaves

4 slices bacon

Stuffing

2 garlic cloves, crushed

1 onion, finely diced

leaves from 4 sprigs of thyme

1 large potato, coarsely grated

10 oz. fresh sausage meat

juice and zest of 1 unwaxed lemon

sea salt and freshly ground black pepper

Gravy

2 tablespoons plain flour

2 cups chicken stock

sea salt and freshly ground black pepper

For me, the smell of roasting chicken conjures up childhood memories of a cozy Sunday at home, so now I often cook it for my own family. It's always worth cooking a larger bird than you need because the leftovers can be used in a pilaf or to make sandwiches. You can also use the carcass to make stock, and freeze it for making soup or risotto. Three meals for the price of one bird!

Preheat the oven to 350°F. Lightly oil a roasting pan.

Take the chicken and carefully slide your hand between the skin and the breast meat. Insert the lemon slices under the skin along with the bay leaves.

To make the stuffing, put the garlic, onion, thyme, potato and sausage meat in a large bowl. Add the lemon zest and juice, season, and mix well. Cut any excess fat from the cavity of the chicken, then stuff the bird with the potato mixture.

Weigh your chicken to work out the cooking time: you should allow 20 minutes per pound, plus 20 minutes extra. Put the chicken in the prepared roasting pan and lay the bacon over the breast. Put in the hot oven and cook for the time you have calculated. When the chicken is ready, remove it from the roasting pan and keep warm.

Now make the gravy. Add the flour to the pan and stir with a wooden spoon to combine with the fat and juices. Slowly pour in the chicken stock, stirring continuously to prevent lumps forming. Place the roasting pan directly over the heat and bring to a boil. When the mixture has thickened, remove it from the heat and season well. If you like a very smooth gravy, press it through a strainer with the back of a spoon.

Carve the chicken and serve with the stuffing, a selection of trimmings (see page 100), and the hot gravy.

butterflied leg of lamb with mediterranean stuffing

Preparation 30 minutes
Cooking 1 hours 30 minutes
Serves 6

3½-lb. leg of lamb, butterflied
Stuffing
leaves from 2 sprigs of rosemary
2 red onions, finely chopped
3 garlic cloves, finely chopped
½ cup pitted olives, chopped
1 zucchini, grated and squeezed dry
1 egg
1 tablespoon olive oil
sea salt and freshly ground black pepper
Gravy
2 tablespoons flour
1 teaspoon tomato concentrate
3 tablespoons red currant jelly
⅓ cup red wine
1 cup vegetable stock
sea salt and freshly ground black pepper

Your butcher will butterfly the leg of lamb for you, but if you want to do it yourself, hold a very sharp knife like a dagger and cut from the fleshy end of the leg to the opposite end. Then let your knife follow the bones, cutting the flesh away so that the meat opens out like a butterfly.

Preheat the oven to 375°F. Lighly oil a roasting pan.

Combine all the stuffing ingredients and season. Open out the leg of lamb, skin-side down, and spread the stuffing over it. Fold the lamb back together and tie securely with string. Place the lamb in the prepared pan and roast for 1 hour and 20 minutes. When cooked, transfer the lamb to a carving plate and keep warm.

Pour half the fat out of the roasting pan, add the flour, and mix until smooth. Stir in the tomato concentrate and red currant jelly, then pour in the wine and stock, mixing thoroughly. Place the pan directly over the heat and stir constantly until the gravy thickens. Adjust the seasoning and press the gravy through a strainer to remove any lumps. Cut the string from the lamb and carve. Serve with mashed potatoes and steamed green beans.

roast pork
with baked stuffed apples

Preparation 20 minutes

Cooking 1 hour 30 minutes

Serves 6

3½-lb. pork loin, boned and rolled

3 eating apples

1 onion, chopped

8 fresh sage leaves, chopped

1 tablespoon olive oil

sea salt and freshly ground black pepper

Gravy

2 tablespoons flour

1 cup white wine

1 cup vegetable stock

sea salt and freshly ground black pepper

The combination of pork and apple is a classic one, but it's given a twist in this recipe by stuffing the apples with onion and fresh sage.

Preheat the oven to 425°F. Lightly oil a roasting pan.

Dry the pork with paper towels, place in the prepared pan, and roast for 30 minutes. Reduce the heat to 350°F and cook the pork for a further 30 minutes.

Slice the apples in half across the middle and cut out the core. Mix the onion and sage with the oil and season. Arrange the apple halves around the roasting pork and fill the cavities with the stuffing. Return to the oven and cook for 30 minutes. When cooked, transfer the pork and apples to a carving plate and keep warm.

To make the gravy, drain half the fat from the roasting pan, add the flour, and mix until smooth. Pour in the wine and stock and mix thoroughly. Place the roasting pan directly over the heat and keep stirring until the gravy thickens. Adjust the seasoning. For a very smooth gravy, press it through a strainer. Serve the pork with the roast apples, a selection of vegetables (see page 100), and the gravy.

roast duck with citrus fruits

Preparation 15 minutes
Cooking 2 hours 30 minutes
Serves 4

1 x 7-lb. duck
1 unwaxed lemon, thinly sliced
1 unwaxed orange, thinly sliced
1 unwaxed lime, thinly sliced
Orange sauce
1 tablespoon flour
$2/3$ cup vegetable stock
$2/3$ cup orange juice
sea salt and freshly ground black pepper

Duck has a wonderful flavor, but it is a fatty meat, so this recipe contains citrus fruit to help cut through the richness. Do not be alarmed at the size of the duck specified; it loses a huge amount of fat during cooking, and has much less meat than a chicken of the same size.

Preheat the oven to 375°F. Lightly grease a roasting pan.

Put all the slices of citrus fruit in the cavity of the duck. Rub seasoning all over the skin. Place the duck on a roasting rack in the prepared pan; this is important so that the fat can drip out and the duck will not be sitting in it. Place in the oven and roast for 2½ hours.

When cooked, lift up the duck and pour the juices from the cavity into a heatproof pitcher. Transfer the duck to a carving plate and keep warm while making the sauce.

To make the orange sauce, drain all but 1 tablespoon of fat from the roasting pan (save the excess in the fridge for general cooking purposes). Add the flour to the pan and mix thoroughly. Stir in the stock and orange juice, and add the reserved duck juices. Place over the heat and bring to a boil, stirring constantly. If you want a very smooth sauce, press the mixture through a strainer. Carve the duck and serve with carrots, roast potatoes, and the orange sauce.

sunday dinner trimmings

Every good roast needs the traditional accompaniments to take it to the next level of deliciousness. All the ideas below serve 4.

roast potatoes

12–16 potatoes, peeled
4 tablespoons duck or goose fat or olive oil

Preheat the oven to 350°F. Parboil the potatoes for 12 minutes, drain, and shake in the colander to roughen up the outsides. Heat the fat in a large roasting pan in the oven. When very hot, carefully add the potatoes, turning to coat them in the hot oil. Return to the oven and cook for 40 minutes. Do not disturb them before that or you will spoil their chances of crisping up. Turn them and cook for a further 20 minutes.

roast sesame beets, parsnips, and carrots

1½ tablespoons butter
2 tablespoons olive oil
6 oz. each beetroot, parsnips, and carrots, peeled and chopped
2 tablespoons sesame seeds

Preheat the oven to 350°F. Heat the butter and oil in a roasting pan, add the vegetables, and toss to coat. Put in the oven and roast for 35 minutes. Remove and turn with a spoon to ensure even cooking. Sprinkle with the sesame seeds and return to the oven for a further 20 minutes.

cauliflower with cheese sauce

1 cauliflower, cut into florets
2 tablespoons butter
3 tablespoons flour
2½ cups milk
6 oz. Cheddar or other hard cheese, grated

Preheat the oven to 350°F. Steam the cauliflower over a pan of boiling water for 5 minutes. Melt the butter in a small saucepan, stir in the flour to make a smooth paste, then add the milk. Stir constantly until it thickens, then add all but ½ cup of the cheese, stirring until it has melted. Place the cauliflower in a buttered ovenproof dish and pour the sauce over it. Top with the remaining cheese and bake for 25 minutes.

steamed vegetables

Choose two or three vegetables for a Sunday dinner, allowing about 3–4 oz. per person. Steam over a pan of boiling water for 3–4 minutes and serve lightly seasoned and tossed in a little olive oil or butter.

gravy variations

Follow the basic gravy method described on page 92, using the appropriate stock mixed half and half with wine or vegetable water if you wish.

Beef—add 1 teaspoon mild mustard.

Chicken—add the juice of 1 lemon.

Duck—substitute ½ cup stock with cranberry, orange, or cherry juice.

Lamb—melt ½ cup red currant jelly in the microwave and substitute for some of the liquid.

Pork—add 1 teaspoon mild mustard or a dash of soy sauce, or substitute ½ cup of the stock with the same quantity of apple juice or cider.

In the summer serve any of these roasts with green sauce (see page 118) for a Mediterranean-flavored meal.

fish and shrimp kedgeree

Preparation 20 minutes
Cooking 40 minutes
Serves 4

1½ cups brown basmati rice
12 oz. undyed smoked haddock
3 tablespoons butter
1 tablespoon oil
2 shallots, diced
6½ oz. cooked peeled shrimp
a handful of fresh parsley, finely chopped
4 hard-cooked eggs, quartered
4 lemon wedges
sea salt and freshly ground black pepper

Originally an Indian dish, kedgeree was appropriated by the British during the days of the empire. It makes a good brunch dish.

Wash and cook the rice according to the package instructions, then drain and place in a large bowl.

Preheat the oven to 350°F. Put the fish on a piece of foil, wrap loosely, and place on a baking sheet in the oven for 10 minutes. When cooked and cool enough to handle, flake the fish onto the cooked rice.

Heat the butter and oil in a pan, add the shallots, and sauté for 3 minutes. Add the shrimp and sauté for a further 2 minutes. Mix into the rice, season, and add all but 1 tablespoon of the parsley. Transfer to a serving bowl.

Arrange the eggs on top of the rice, add the lemon wedges, and scatter with the remaining parsley.

chicken in a pot

Preparation 20 minutes
Cooking 1 hour 15 minutes
Serves 4–6

1 medium free-range chicken
2 celery ribs, chopped
1 red onion, chopped
2 garlic cloves, finely sliced
3 carrots, chopped
1 turnip, about 6 oz., chopped
2 bay leaves
1 sprig of rosemary
2 sprigs of thyme
8 small waxy potatoes
½ head of Savoy cabbage
sea salt and freshly ground black pepper

King Henry IV said that every family in France should be given the ingredients to make this dish once a week. Sound advice, as it's good-value family fare.

Cut any excess fat or skin off the chicken and place the bird in a large Dutch oven. Add the celery, onion, garlic, carrots, turnip, herbs, and seasoning. Add just enough water to cover, then place over the heat and bring to a boil. Reduce to a simmer, then cover and cook for 45 minutes. Add the potatoes and cook for a further 25 minutes. Spoon off any excess fat floating on top of the liquid. Trim the cabbage and cut into 4 wedges, add to the pot, cover, and cook for 4 minutes.

Remove the chicken, cut into pieces, and serve, ladling over the vegetables and stock at the table.

family and friends

Eating together with family and friends is one of life's great pleasures. Good food and conversation seem to go hand in hand, so it's great to cook up some favorite dishes and have a variety of generations sitting around the table and enjoying a fine meal that everyone has contributed to preparing.

To make life easier, the recipes in this section include several one-pot dishes, such as cassoulet and baked ham with layered potatoes, and perennial family favorites, such as meatloaf and burgers. When you're surrounded by loved ones, the food doesn't have to be grand—it just needs to be tasty, nutritious, and abundant. The following recipes are just that.

chicken and bacon pot

Preparation 10 minutes
Cooking 45 minutes
Serves 4

1 tablespoon olive oil
10 oz. thick bacon, diced
8 oz. button mushrooms
4 chicken breasts
1 garlic clove, crushed
2 shallots, diced
1/3 cup flour
2 cups chicken stock
1 cup white wine
1 bay leaf
a handful of fresh parsley, chopped
sea salt and freshly ground black pepper

The bacon adds a special intensity to the flavor of this easy-to-make dish. Serve with rice to mop up the lovely sauce.

Heat the olive oil in a flameproof casserole dish, add the bacon and mushrooms, and cook over medium heat until golden. Transfer to a plate.

Put the chicken breasts in the casserole and quickly brown on both sides. Set aside with the bacon. Preheat the oven to 350°F.

Sauté the garlic and shallots over low heat in the same pan for 5 minutes. Add the flour and mix well. Remove the pan from the heat, slowly pour in the stock and wine, and stir until smooth. Return to the heat and bring to a boil, stirring constantly. Mix in the bacon and mushrooms, then add the chicken breasts, bay leaf, and seasoning. Cover and cook in the oven for 30 minutes. Add the parsley just before serving.

mediterranean garlic shrimp

Preparation 40 minutes
Cooking 5 minutes
Serves 4

4 lb. uncooked shrimp, shells on, or 2 1/4 lb. uncooked shrimp, shelled and deveined
3 tablespoons olive oil
3 tablespoons butter
3 garlic cloves, crushed
a bunch of fresh parsley, chopped
juice of 1 lemon
sea salt and freshly ground black pepper

Fantastically quick and easy to prepare, and a great favorite at family gatherings. Serve with a mixed salad and lots of crusty bread.

If using unshelled shrimp, run a small, sharp knife down the back of each one and remove the black vein. Put the shrimp in a colander, rinse well, and drain thoroughly.

Heat the oil and butter in a large pan, add the garlic and shrimp, and cook for 3 minutes on high heat, tossing well. The shrimp are cooked through when they are totally pink all over. Add the parsley, lemon juice, and seasoning, toss well, and serve with plenty of warm bread for mopping up the yummy juices.

baked ham with layered potatoes

Preparation 30 minutes + 1 hour soaking
Cooking 1 hour 20 minutes
Serves 6

2-lb. boneless ham joint
2 lb. potatoes, peeled and thinly sliced
1–2 onions, thinly sliced
1 cup hot chicken or ham stock
2 tablespoons butter, melted
sea salt and freshly ground black pepper

a shallow ovenproof dish, 8 inches in diameter, buttered

Family meals don't come much simpler than this. For easier carving, ask your butcher to bone the ham joint for you.

Preheat the oven to 400°F.

If the ham joint is salty, cover it in cold water and leave to soak for 1 hour. Drain and pat dry with paper towels. Wrap the ham loosely in foil and put in a roasting pan. Bake for 1 hour 20 minutes (40 minutes per pound).

Meanwhile, put a layer of potatoes (overlapping slightly) in the prepared dish, top with a layer of onions and season with salt and pepper. Continue making layers, finishing with a layer of the potatoes. Push the layers down firmly with the palms of your hands. Pour the hot stock into the dish, brush the top with melted butter, and cover with foil.

Bake the potatoes at the top of the oven with the ham for 50 minutes, then remove the foil and continue to cook for a further 30 minutes. The top should be golden brown and crunchy and the potatoes soft when a knife is inserted.

meatloaf with two sauces

Preparation 30 minutes
Cooking 1 hour 15 minutes
Serves 6

12 slices prosciutto

6 oz. chicken livers, chopped

14 oz. lean pork, diced

10 oz. ground turkey or chicken

1 red onion, diced

2 eggs, beaten

3 bay leaves, torn

a bunch of fresh flat-leaf parsley, chopped

sea salt and freshly ground black pepper

Tomato sauce and spiced tomato sauce

3 tablespoons olive oil

1 onion, diced

2 garlic cloves, crushed

2 x 14-oz. cans chopped tomatoes

1 red chile, chopped

a 9 x 5-inch loaf pan

In France the humble meatloaf is called a "terrine," which makes it sound a lot grander. Here it's served with two tomato sauces, one of which is spiced up for more adventurous eaters.

Preheat the oven to 325°F.

Line the loaf pan with the prosciutto, leaving some aside to cover the top of the finished meatloaf.

Put the chicken livers in a bowl with the pork and turkey, add the onion, eggs, bay leaves, and parsley, then season and mix well. This is best done with your hands.

Fill the prepared pan with the meat, flatten out the top, and cover with the remaining prosciutto. Cover with foil and bake in the oven for 1 hour 15 minutes. Remove and let stand for 10 minutes. Drain off any juice into a pitcher, then turn out the meatloaf onto a deep plate.

To make the tomato sauce, heat the oil and sauté the onion gently for 5 minutes. Add the garlic and cook for a further 5 minutes. Add the tomatoes and reserved meat juices, season, and simmer gently for 30 minutes, stirring frequently.

To make the spiced tomato sauce, pour half the tomato mixture into another pan, add the chopped chile, and simmer for 10 minutes. Serve both sauces with the meatloaf.

homemade burgers

Preparation 30 minutes
Cooking 10 minutes
Makes 4

20 oz. lean ground beef
1 garlic clove, crushed
1 shallot, finely diced
a bunch of fresh parsley, chopped
1 teaspoon Worcestershire sauce
olive oil, for frying
4 slices streaky bacon
2 small ciabatta loaves
4 tablespoons mayonnaise
4 tomato slices
1 cup grated sharp Cheddar cheese
1 avocado, sliced
4 leaves iceberg lettuce, shredded
sea salt and freshly ground black pepper

Burgers are fantastically versatile, so build yours just as you wish, with or without the suggested garnishes.

Put the beef, garlic, shallot, parsley, and Worcestershire sauce in a large bowl, season, and mix well with your hands. Divide the mixture into four and shape into burgers.

Heat some olive oil in a large frying pan and cook for 2 minutes on each side for rare, 3 minutes for medium-rare, and 4 minutes for well done.

Meanwhile, grill the bacon until crisp. Cut the ciabatta rolls in half and toast the insides. Spread the toasted sides with mayonnaise. Put a slice of tomato on the toasted base and a burger on top, followed by a handful of cheese, if using, a bacon rasher, a slice or two of avocado, and some lettuce. Sandwich together with the remaining bread and serve with ketchup and mustard.

cassoulet

Preparation 30 minutes
+ overnight soaking
Cooking 3 hours 30 minutes
Serves 4–6

1½ cups dried white beans
1 onion
1 carrot
4 tomatoes
1 bay leaf
1 sprig of thyme
a bunch of fresh parsley
1 celery rib
14 oz. duck confit
4 Toulouse sausages
6 oz. pork loin, chopped
10 oz. lamb stewing meat, cubed
2 garlic cloves, slightly crushed
2 cups breadcrumbs
sea salt and freshly ground black pepper

Although this famous French dish takes a while to make, it is well worth the effort. Any leftovers reheat well, so why not make a double quantity?

Soak the haricot beans overnight in a bowl of water. Drain and place in a saucepan, cover with fresh water, and add the onion, carrot, and tomatoes. Bring to a boil.

Meanwhile, tie the bay leaf, thyme, parsley, and celery together with string (this makes removal easier) and add to the beans. Stir well and cook for 1½ hours, until the beans are soft. Add more water if needed while cooking, always keeping 1 inch of liquid above the beans.

Heat a little of the fat from the duck confit and brown the sausages in it. Set aside on a plate. Put the pork and lamb in the pan and cook over high heat to seal the outside. When the beans are cooked, drain any excess liquid into the meat, and simmer for 30 minutes.

Meanwhile, preheat the oven to 350°F. Rub the inside of a large Dutch oven with the garlic and leave both cloves in the dish.

Discard the vegetables and herbs from the beans. Put a layer of beans in the prepared pan, arrange all the meat, including the duck confit, on top, and cover with the remaining beans. Pour in as much cooking liquid as the pan will hold, then sprinkle with a layer of breadcrumbs. Place in the oven and cook for 1½ hours, stirring every 20 minutes and topping with a fresh layer of breadcrumbs (these help to thicken the cooking liquid).

When ready, the final breadcrumb topping should be golden, with the juices bubbling up around the edges. Serve with a simple green salad.

sauces

Extra flavor and complexity can be added to savory dishes by serving them with an additional sauce. Here are some ideas.

mustard mayo

Great with new potatoes and burgers, and for dunking fries.

Preparation 20 minutes
Makes enough for 4

2 egg yolks
2 teaspoons Dijon mustard
1 teaspoon English mustard
2 teaspoons white wine vinegar
1 garlic clove, crushed to a paste
1¼ cups olive oil
sea salt and freshly ground black pepper

Put the egg yolks, mustards, vinegar, and garlic in a bowl, and mix well. Season, add a drop of oil, and mix again. Continue adding the oil a drop at a time, mixing after each addition; this will prevent the mayo curdling. Adjust the seasoning if necessary. Store in the fridge until needed.

hollandaise sauce

This is traditionally served with fish and steamed vegetables.

Preparation 20 minutes
Makes enough for 4

2 sticks butter
2 egg yolks
1 tablespoon white wine vinegar
sea salt and fine white pepper

Melt the butter in a small saucepan. Put the egg yolks in a small heatproof bowl and whisk with a hand-held blender. Continue blending very slowly as you pour in the butter so that the mixture emulsifies. Add the vinegar and seasoning, and blend again. Put plastic wrap directly on top of the sauce to prevent a skin forming. Place the bowl in a saucepan of hot water for 10 minutes, or until needed.

harissa

Use this spicy Moroccan sauce with couscous or roast meats.

Preparation 30 minutes
Cooking 1 hour
Makes enough for 6–8

⅔ cup olive oil
2 red onions, chopped
5 garlic cloves, crushed
1 teaspoon ground cumin seeds
1 teaspoon ground fennel seeds
1 teaspoon ground coriander seeds
3 roasted red peppers, peeled, seeded, and chopped
6 medium-hot red chiles, seeded and chopped

Heat the oil in a pan and gently sauté the onions and garlic without coloring for 10 minutes. Add the seeds and cook for a few minutes. Stir in the peppers and chiles and simmer for 10 minutes. Transfer to a blender or food processor and blitz until smooth. Return to the pan and cook very slowly for a further 30 minutes. Remove and let cool. Store in the fridge, topped with olive oil, for up to 3 weeks.

charmoula

A Middle Eastern sauce served with broiled fish and meat.

Preparation 25 minutes + 1 hour steeping
Makes enough for 4

4 tablespoons olive oil
2 tablespoons wine vinegar
2 tablespoons honey
2 garlic cloves, crushed
1 red chile, finely diced
2 teaspoons cumin
2 teaspoons paprika
a bunch of fresh flat-leaf parsley, finely chopped
5 scallions, thinly sliced
⅓ cup raisins
2 carrots, finely grated
sea salt and freshly ground black pepper

Combine the olive oil, vinegar, and honey in a bowl, then stir in the garlic, chile, cumin, and paprika. Add the parsley, scallions, raisins, and carrots, season and mix well, then let stand for 1 hour before serving.

red chile sauce

A medium-hot sauce that will add a kick to all savory dishes.

Preparation 10 minutes
Cooking 30 minutes
Makes enough for 4

4 garlic cloves, crushed
4 red chiles, chopped
½ cup sugar

Put the garlic and chiles in a small pan, cover with 1 cup water and bring to a simmer. Cook for 30 minutes, checking the water level frequently and adding more if needed. Remove from the heat and stir in the sugar. Blitz with a hand-held blender until smooth and let cool before using.

green sauce

The vibrant color of this sauce comes from the herbs it contains. It is often used on pasta, and is also good with barbecued meats and fish.

Preparation 30 minutes
Makes enough for 4

a bunch of fresh parsley, finely chopped
a bunch of fresh cilantro, finely chopped
a bunch of fresh dill, finely chopped
a bunch of fresh watercress, chopped
1 tablespoon capers, finely chopped
2 garlic cloves, crushed
6 tablespoons olive oil
sea salt and freshly ground black pepper

Put all the herbs in a bowl with the watercress, capers, and garlic, and mix well. Drizzle in the olive oil, season, and mix again.

gremolata

An Italian sauce that usually accompanies *osso bucco* (stewed shin of veal), but it also goes well with lamb and other meats.

Preparation 10 minutes
Makes enough for 4

3 garlic cloves, finely chopped
a large bunch of parsley, finely chopped
zest and juice of 2 unwaxed lemons
6 tablespoons olive oil
sea salt and freshly ground black pepper

Put all the ingredients in a bowl and mix well. The texture should be fine. In fact, the more finely chopped the ingredients, the better the sauce.

tartar sauce

A mayonnaise-type sauce usually served with fish. Why not try it with fries or jacket potatoes too?

Preparation 20 minutes
Makes enough for 4

2 egg yolks
½ teaspoon English mustard powder
¾ cup olive oil
juice of 1 lemon
1 tablespoon capers, chopped
1 tablespoon gherkins, chopped
1 shallot, chopped
1 tablespoon parsley, chopped
sea salt and freshly ground black pepper

Put the egg and mustard powder in a bowl and whisk together. Drizzle in the olive oil very slowly, whisking constantly. Add the lemon juice and mix well. Stir in the capers, gherkins, shallot, and parsley, season and mix again. Refrigerate if not using right away.

hot and sour sauce

This exotic sauce is a good dip for shrimp and chicken, and can also be used to dress an Asian salad.

Preparation 20 minutes
Cooking 30 minutes
Makes enough for 4

6 medium-sized green chiles, seeded and chopped
juice of 4 limes
4-inch piece galangal or fresh ginger, peeled and chopped
a pinch of sea salt

Put the chiles in a small saucepan, and add the lime juice, galangal, and salt. Add just enough water to cover and bring to a simmer. Bubble gentle for 30 minutes, adding more water if needed.

Blitz with a hand-held blender to make a smoothish sauce. Taste and adjust the seasoning, if necessary, and consistency if you wish.

sweet treats

We hear a lot about the incidence of obesity these days and that's
something we certainly don't want to contribute to. None of us
wants to be fat, or cause our loved ones to gain an unhealthy
amount of weight. But that doesn't mean we can't have the
occasional sweet treat. As with most things in life, moderation
is the watchword.

This section starts with cakes and cookies, which most people
can enjoy with a clear conscience from time to time. I've tried
to maximize the healthy ingredients in them, using unrefined
products whenever possible. This means that they release their
energy slowly rather than giving an instant rush that can lead
to craving more and more sugar.

The pies and puddings follow similar principles, aiming to
combine the best ingredients with the most delicious flavors.
Your family will love them all!

english flapjacks

These chewy oat bars are a lovely treat to slip into a lunch box.

Preparation 10 minutes
Cooking 20 minutes
Makes 8

13 tablespoons butter
1 tablespoon golden syrup or maple syrup
1 scant cup packed brown sugar
2 cups old-fashioned rolled oats

a shallow baking pan, 8 x 12 inches, lined with parchment

Preheat the oven to 300°F.

Melt the butter in a large saucepan, add the syrup and sugar, and stir until the sugar has dissolved. Remove from the heat and stir in the oats. Spoon the mixture into the prepared baking pan and bake for 20 minutes. When done, cut into squares and let cool.

honeyjacks

A healthy and sustaining snack that keeps you going for hours.

Preparation 10 minutes
Cooking 20 minutes
Makes 8

13 tablespoons butter
1 tablespoon golden syrup or maple syrup
½ cup packed brown sugar
⅓ cup honey
2 cups old-fashioned rolled oats
⅓ cup raisins
1 cup shredded coconut

a shallow baking pan, 8 x 12 inches, lined with parchment

Preheat the oven to 300°F.

Melt the butter in a large saucepan, add the syrup, sugar, and honey, and stir until the sugar has dissolved. Remove from the heat and stir in the oats and raisins. Spoon the mixture into the prepared baking pan, sprinkle with the coconut, and bake for 20 minutes. When done, cut into squares and let cool before eating.

nutty jacks

Nuts are high in protein and fiber, so they are a healthy addition to flapjacks.

Preparation 10 minutes
Cooking 20 minutes
Makes 8

13 tablespoons butter
1 tablespoon golden syrup or maple syrup
1 scant cup packed brown sugar
2 cups old-fashioned rolled oats
⅓ cup chopped nuts
4–6 oz. semisweet chocolate, melted

a shallow baking pan, 8 x 12 inches, lined with parchment

Preheat the oven to 300°F.

Melt the butter in a large saucepan, add the syrup and sugar, and stir until the sugar has dissolved. Remove from the heat and stir in the oats and nuts. Spoon the mixture into the prepared baking pan, place in the oven, and bake for 20 minutes. When done, cut into squares and let cool. Drizzle the melted chocolate over the nutty jacks in a zigzag pattern and allow to set.

oat and chocolate cookies

My friend Rebecca, who loves to cook, gave me the recipe for these much-loved cookies. They're a staple treat in my family.

Preparation 20 minutes
Cooking 20 minutes
Makes 15–20

2 sticks (16 tablespoons) butter, softened
1/4 cup granulated sugar
1/2 cup packed light brown sugar
4 oz. semisweeet chocolate chips
1 3/4 cups old-fashioned rolled oats
1 1/2 cups self-rising flour

Preheat the oven to 350°F.

Cream together the butter and sugars. Stir in the chocolate chips and oats. Add the flour and mix well.

Using your hands, form the mixture into 15–20 small balls. Flatten them slightly with your palms and place them on a baking sheet, allowing room for spreading. Bake in the oven for 15–20 minutes.

When done, cool on a wire rack and store in an airtight container.

shortbread

A classic three-ingredient cookie, ideal for children to help make. Take care that the flour is not overmixed or the finished dough will be tough.

Preparation 15 minutes
Cooking 45 minutes
Makes 16

14 tablespoons butter, softened
1/2 cup granulated sugar, plus extra for sprinkling
2 1/4 cups flour

a loose-bottomed baking pan, 8 inches square, lightly buttered

Preheat the oven to 300°F.

Cream the butter and sugar together until light and smooth. Add the flour and mix quickly with the back of a wooden spoon until the mixture resembles breadcrumbs.

Tip the mixture into the prepared baking pan. Flatten evenly with the back of a spoon and sprinkle with a little extra sugar. Bake for 45 minutes.

When done, remove from the oven and let cool for 5 minutes, before cutting into 16 squares. Store in an airtight container.

pumpkin seed cookies

Seeds contain lots of nutrients that are an important part of a good diet. A great way to feed them to your family is to hide them in cookies, and these ones are really quick and easy to make.

Preparation 20 minutes
Cooking 12–15 minutes
Makes 20

1 1/2 cups self-rising flour
1 stick (8 tablespoons) butter, diced
2/3 cup light brown sugar
1 egg, beaten
1/2 cup pumpkin seeds

Preheat the oven to 350°F.

Put the flour, butter, and sugar in a bowl and mix with a fork until the mixure resembles breadcrumbs. Add the egg and seeds, mix again, and form into a ball. Lightly flour a work surface and use your hands to roll the dough into a sausage shape about 8 inches long. Cut into 20 slices and place on a nonstick or buttered baking sheet. Bake for 12–15 minutes.

When done, cool on a wire rack, then store in an airtight container.

basic cake

Preparation 45 minutes
Cooking 35–45 minutes

2½ sticks (20 tablespoons) margarine
1½ cups natural cane sugar
5 eggs
1 teaspoon pure vanilla extract
2¾ cups self-rising flour
1 teaspoon baking powder
Icing
1½ cups confectioners' sugar
juice of 1 lemon

a shallow baking pan, 8 x 12 inches, lined with baking parchment

This is a light, moist sponge cake that can be dressed up or down to suit any family occasion.

Preheat the oven to 350°F. Put the margarine and cane sugar in a bowl and mix until light and fluffy. Beat in the eggs, then stir in the vanilla extract. Sift in the flour and baking powder, then fold together quickly with a large spoon (speed at this stage keeps the cake light). Spoon the mixture into the prepared baking pan, place in the middle of the oven, and bake for 30–35 minutes. When done, a knife inserted in the center of the cake should come out clean; if it doesn't, cook for a further 5–10 minutes. Cool in the pan for 5 minutes, then turn out onto a wire rack and let cool completely.

To make the icing, sift the confectioners' sugar into a bowl and stir in the lemon juice. Carefully add a little water to make a smooth, stiff paste. Place the cake on a plate and use a wet narrow spatula to spread the icing over the top. Decorate with sweets or berries if you wish, then allow to set before serving.

lemon polenta cake

Preparation 20 minutes
Cooking 30 minutes

1½ sticks (12 tablespoons) butter, softened
¾ cup natural cane sugar
¾ cup polenta or cornmeal
½ teaspoon baking powder
1 cup ground almonds
zest and juice of 1 unwaxed lemon
½ teaspoon pure vanilla extract
3 eggs
Syrup
zest and juice of 2 unwaxed lemons
¼ cup natural cane sugar

a springform cake pan, 10 inches in diameter, lightly greased

Polenta, or cornmeal, gives a slighter coarser texture than wheat flour, but is still delicious.

Preheat the oven to 350°F. Beat together the butter and sugar until creamy. Add the polenta, baking powder, ground almonds, lemon zest and juice, vanilla extract, and eggs. Mix until smooth. Spoon the mixture into the prepared pan and bake in the middle of the oven for 30 minutes.

Meanwhile, make the syrup. Put the lemon zest and juice in a small saucepan with the sugar and 2 tablespoons water. Bring to a boil and simmer for 2 minutes. When the cake is done, let cool slightly in the pan, then turn out and pierce all over with a fine skewer. Spoon the syrup over the cake, then let stand for 20 minutes while it is absorbed. Serve with crème fraîche.

devil's food cake

Preparation 30 minutes
Cooking 25 minutes

127.5g 6½ tablespoons butter
125ml ½ cup packed light brown sugar
6 tablespoons golden syrup or corn syrup
~80ml 1 cup + 2 tablespoons all-purpose flour
¼ cup cocoa powder
1 egg, beaten
1 teaspoon baking soda
125ml ½ cup milk
Frosting
3 tablespoons cocoa powder
3 tablespoons hot water
6½ tablespoons butter, softened
1¼ cups confectioners' sugar
1 tablespoon golden syrup or corn syrup
2 drops pure vanilla extract

2 cake pans, 8 inches in diameter, greased

Wickedly rich and chocolatey, this cake will have everyone clamoring for more.

Preheat the oven to 350°F. *180°C*

Put the butter, sugar, and golden syrup in a saucepan and heat gently until the sugar has dissolved.

Sift the flour and cocoa into a bowl, add the sugar mixture, and stir well. Add the egg and mix again. Combine the baking soda with the milk, add to the bowl, and mix thoroughly. Divide the mixture between the prepared cake pans and smooth out with a narrow spatula. Place in the oven and bake for 20 minutes, until just firm to the touch. Turn onto a wire rack to cool.

To make the frosting, put the cocoa in a bowl and mix in the hot water. Add the butter, sugar, golden syrup, and vanilla extract and beat until smooth.

When the cakes are cold, sandwich together with some of the frosting. (Dip your narrow spatula in hot water to prevent the frosting sticking to it.) Spread the remainder over the top and sides of the cake, making the surface as smooth or ruffled as you wish.

carrot cake

Preparation 30 minutes
Cooking 1 hour

4 eggs, separated
1 cup packed brown sugar
zest and juice of 1 unwaxed orange
1²/₃ cups ground walnuts
1 teaspoon ground cinnamon
1½ cups grated carrot
¾ cup whole wheat flour
1 teaspoon baking powder
Frosting
8 oz. cream cheese
²/₃ cup confectioners' sugar
zest and juice of 1 small unwaxed orange

*a loose-bottomed cake pan,
8 inches square, greased*

A scrumptious teatime treat—no wonder it's also known as "passion cake" in England!

Preheat the oven to 350°F.

Put the egg yolks and sugar in a bowl and whisk until thick and creamy. Add all the remaining ingredients, except the egg whites, and fold carefully until the mixture is smooth.

Whisk the egg whites until stiff, then fold into the cake mixture. Pour into the prepared cake pan and bake in the center of the oven for 1 hour. When done, cool in the pan for 5 minutes, then turn out and cool completely on a wire rack.

To make the frosting, cream the cheese and confectioners' sugar together. Add a little orange zest and juice to flavor. Spread over the top of the cold cake using a narrow spatula dipped in hot water. Sprinkle with the remaining orange zest.

banana cake

Preparation 20 minutes
Cooking 1 hour

¾ cup natural cane sugar
1 tablespoon golden syrup or corn syrup
¾ cup vegetable oil
2 eggs
2 ripe bananas
1 teaspoon pure vanilla extract
2¼ cups self-rising flour
1 teaspoon baking powder

a 9 x 5-inch loaf pan, lightly greased

In my family this cake is popular even with those who don't like bananas. The flavor improves with keeping, so wrap the cake in plastic wrap and keep for a couple of days before cutting.

Preheat the oven to 350°F.

Put the sugar and syrup in a bowl. Put the oil, eggs, bananas, and vanilla extract in another bowl and whiz with a hand-held blender. Add to the bowl of sugar and mix until smooth. Fold in the flour and baking powder, then spoon into the prepared pan. Bake in the middle of the oven for 50–60 minutes. When it is done, a knife inserted in the center of the cake should come out clean.

seasonal fruit tray tart

Preparation 30 minutes
Cooking 45 minutes
Serves 6

1 lb. frozen puff pastry dough, thawed
2 lb. seasonal fruit, such as apples, apricots, nectarines, peaches, or plums, cored or pitted, as necessary
1 egg, beaten
¼ cup natural cane sugar
3 tablespoons butter
honey, for drizzling
confectioners' sugar, for dusting

A simple dessert that makes the most of any fruit in season. Serve with whipped cream or crème fraîche for a special treat.

Preheat the oven to 350°F. Lightly grease a baking sheet.

Unfold the pastry and place on the prepared baking sheet. Arrange the fruit on the pastry in an even layer, leaving a 1½-inch border around the edges. Brush the border with the egg and fold inwards all the way around. Sprinkle the fruit with the cane sugar and dot with the butter. Place in the oven and bake for 45 minutes, reducing the heat if the pastry shows signs of burning. Drizzle with honey and dust with confectioners' sugar before serving.

chocolate swamp pudding

Preparation 30 minutes
Cooking 25 minutes
Serves 4

6½ tablespoons butter
½ cup natural cane sugar
½ cup milk
2 eggs
1 teaspoon pure vanilla extract
1 cup self-rising flour
½ cup cocoa powder
Chocolate swamp
¾ cup + 2 tablespoons packed brown sugar
¼ cup cocoa powder
1 cup boiling water

a 1-quart ovenproof dish, buttered

Melt-in-the-mouth chocolate cake floating in chocolate sauce—this is a dessert to die for.

Preheat the oven to 350°F.

Put the butter, sugar, and milk in a saucepan and heat gently until the sugar has dissolved. Set aside to cool.

Whisk the eggs in a bowl and add the vanilla extract. Sift the flour and cocoa into a large bowl, add the milk and the egg mixture, and stir until smooth. Pour into the prepared baking dish and set aside.

To make the chocolate swamp, mix the sugar and cocoa powder together, then sprinkle evenly over the top of the pudding. Pour on the boiling water and bake in the oven for 25 minutes.

almond fruit crumble

Preparation 30 minutes
Cooking 30 minutes
Serves 4

20 oz. fruit
¼ cup packed brown sugar
1 cup self-rising flour
1 teaspoon baking powder
1 stick (8 tablespoons) butter, diced
¼ cup natural cane sugar
⅓ cup ground almonds
⅓ cup old-fashioned rolled oats

a 1-quart ovenproof dish, buttered

You can't go wrong with a crumble, and the fruit variations are endless. Try rhubarb and ginger, apple and apricot, pear and black currant, or whatever's in the fruit bowl.

Preheat the oven to 375°F. Put the fruit in the prepared dish, add the brown sugar and 6 tablespoons water.

Put the flour, baking powder, and butter in a bowl and rub together with your fingertips until the mixture resembles breadcrumbs. Stir in the cane sugar, almonds, and oats, then spoon evenly over the fruit. Bake in the oven for 30 minutes. The crumble should be golden and the fruit bubbling up around the edges. Serve with custard sauce, cream, or ice cream.

apple and blackberry pie

Preparation 45 minutes
Cooking 40 minutes
Serves 6

2 cups all-purpose flour
1½ sticks (12 tablespoons) butter
⅓ cup natural cane sugar
2 eggs, beaten
Filling
2 lb. apples, peeled and cored
2 pints blackberries
½ cup natural cane sugar

a loose-bottomed tart pan, 10 inches in diameter, lightly buttered

An old favorite that every family should have in its culinary repertoire.

Preheat the oven to 350°F. Put the flour and butter in a bowl and rub together with your fingertips until the mixture resembles breadcrumbs. Stir in the sugar, then add all but 2 tablespoons of the eggs and mix to form a dough. Set aside one-third of the pastry.

Lightly flour a work surface, roll out the larger piece of dough, and use to line the tart pan. Mix the apples, blackberries, and sugar in a bowl and put inside the lined tart pan.

Roll out the smaller piece of dough a little larger than the tart pan. Brush the inside edge of the pastry base with a little of the remaining egg and put the pastry sheet on top of the fruit. Pinch the edges together to seal. Brush the top with the remaining beaten egg, sprinkle with a little sugar, and bake in the oven for 40 minutes, until golden.

pear upside-down dessert

Preparation 30 minutes
Cooking 25 minutes
Serves 6

3 pears, peeled, cored, and halved
6½ tablespoons butter, softened
½ cup natural cane sugar
⅓ cup ground almonds
2 eggs
¾ cup self-rising flour
3 tablespoons cocoa powder
1 teaspoon baking powder
⅓ cup milk
confectioners' sugar, for dusting

a loose-bottomed tart pan, 10 inches in diameter, buttered

A sophisticated-looking dessert that is really easy to make. Any fresh, ripe fruit can be used, but pears are particularly good.

Preheat the oven to 350°F. Arrange the pears in the bottom of the tart pan. Put the butter and sugar in a bowl and cream until smooth. Add the ground almonds and eggs and beat well. Sift in the flour, cocoa, and baking powder, then fold the mixture together. Add the milk and mix until smooth. Cover the pears with the mixture, smoothing it out with a narrow spatula. Bake for 25 minutes.

When done, let cool for 10 minutes, then invert onto a plate. Remove the outer ring of the tart pan, and lift off the base by sliding a narrow spatula underneath it. Dust the cake with confectioners' sugar and serve with whipped cream.

steamed lemon and blueberry pudding

Preparation 25 minutes
Cooking 45 minutes
Serves 6

10 oz. blueberries, fresh or frozen (no need to thaw)
1 stick (8 tablespoons) butter, softened
½ cup + 2 tablespoons sugar
2 eggs
zest and juice of 2 unwaxed lemons
1¼ cups self-rising flour
1 teaspoon baking powder

a 6-cup English pudding bowl, buttered and dusted with sugar

The combination of blueberries and lemon is heavenly: try it and see.

Put the blueberries in the prepared pudding bowl. Cream the butter and sugar together, add the eggs, and beat well. Stir in the lemon zest and juice. Sift in the flour and baking powder and fold into the mixture. Spoon on top of the blueberries and level with the back of a spoon. Cover with a sheet of foil or baking parchment and secure with a rubber band or string.

Quarter fill a large saucepan with hot water, place the pudding bowl in it, then cover and simmer for 45 minutes. Check from time to time, adding more water if necessary. When done, remove the bowl and ease a narrow spatula around the pudding. Invert onto a serving plate, give it a litle shake, then lift off the bowl. Serve with crème fraîche.

crêpes

It's great fun (and less work for you) to set up a "crêpe bar" on the kitchen table and let all the family members help themselves to their favorite topping (see right).

Preparation 15 minutes + 30 minutes chilling
Cooking 10 minutes
Makes 12

¾ cup all-purpose flour
2¼ cups milk
1 large free-range egg
a little butter or vegetable oil, for frying

Put the flour, milk, and egg in a blender or food processor and whiz until smooth. Transfer the mixture to a jug, cover, and chill for 30 minutes. (The batter can be made in advance and kept for up to 24 hours.)

Wipe a frying pan with the butter and heat. Add a ladleful of batter, tilting the pan to spread it evenly. Cook for 1–2 minutes on each side until light brown. Stack the crêpes on a large plate and keep warm. To serve, fold or roll up a crêpe and add the topping of your choice.

crêpe toppings

The simplest ideas are often the best, so here are some quick and easy toppings.

Quick chocolate sauce

5 oz. bittersweeet chocolate
2 tablespoons golden syrup or corn syrup
5 tablespoons unsalted butter
1 tablespoon brandy (optional)

Put all the ingredients in a small saucepan and melt over low heat, stirring continuously until smooth.

Lemon and sugar
The classic way of serving crêpes: squeeze some lemon over the top and sprinkle with a little sugar.

Honey and walnuts
Offer a pot of honey with a drizzler and a little dish of chopped walnuts for scattering.

Fruit jam and cream
Spread good-quality raspberry or strawberry jam on the pancake and top generously with chilled crème fraîche or sour cream.

meringues with baked plums

Preparation 10 minutes
Cooking 1–4 hours
Makes 4–6

3 egg whites
1 cup + 2 tablespoons sugar
16 plums
1 cinnamon stick

a small ovenproof dish with a lid

They look impressive, but meringues are easy to make and the family will love them.

Preheat the oven to 275ºF. Line a baking sheet with baking parchment. Whisk the egg whites until stiff. Add ¾ cup sugar and whisk again until smooth. Place 8 spoonfuls of the mixture on the parchment, spacing them well apart. Bake in the middle of the oven for 1 hour if you like your meringues to have a soft center, or up to 4 hours if you prefer them dry.

Put the plums, cinnamon, and the remaining sugar in the prepared dish, add 3 tablespoons water, and bake with the meringues for 1 hour. Serve together, topped with yogurt.

lemon meringue pie

Preparation 45 minutes
Cooking 45 minutes
Serves 6

zest and juice of 3 unwaxed lemons
1½ cups sugar
½ stick (4 tablespoons) butter
3 tablespoons cornstarch
3 eggs, separated
Pastry
2 cups less 2 tablespoons all-purpose flour
1 stick (8 tablespoons) butter, diced
2 tablespoons sugar
2 eggs, beaten

a loose-bottomed tart pan, 8 inches in diameter, lightly buttered

Crumbly pastry, tangy lemon, and fluffy meringue—the perfect family dessert!

First make the pastry. Put the flour and butter in a bowl and rub together with your fingertips until the mixture resembles breadcrumbs. Add the sugar, then pour in the eggs and mix until you have a dough.

Preheat the oven to 350ºF. Flour a work surface, roll out the dough, and use to line the prepared tart pan. Line the pastry case with baking parchment and fill with baking beans. Bake for 25 minutes. Remove the parchment and beans. Reduce the heat to 300ºF and bake for a further 20 more minutes.

To make the filling, put the lemon zest and juice in a pan, add 1 cup of the sugar, the butter, and cornstarch, and heat gently, stirring constantly until thick. Take off the heat and cool for 10 minutes. Beat in the egg yolks.

For the meringue, whisk the egg whites until stiff, then whisk in the remaining ½ cup sugar. Spoon the lemon filling into the cooked pastry case, top with the meringue, and bake for 15 minutes.

INDEX

A

almond fruit crumble, 134
apples: apple and blackberry
pie, 134
   apple and pear compote, 18
   carrot, apple, and ginger
smoothie, 14
   oat and apple muffins, 26
   roast pork with baked stuffed
apples, 96
asparagus: green bean risotto,
67
avocados: guacamole, 39

B

bacon: chicken and bacon pot,
106
   sausage and bacon toad-in-
the-hole, 61
bagel, classic smoked salmon
37
bananas: banana cake, 130
   banana, pecan, and granola
yogurt pot, 22
   strawberry and banana
smoothie, 17
   whole wheat banana and
chocolate muffins, 27
basic cake, 126
beans: cassoulet, 114
   chili con carne, 78
   chorizo and bean pasties, 50
   kidney bean, egg, and ham
salad, 45
   minestrone with pesto, 73
   sausage and bean soup, 70
beef: beef and carrot casserole,
77
   homemade burgers, 112
   Italian meatballs, 58
   spaghetti bolognese, 78
beets: roast sesame beets,
parsnips, and carrots, 100
blackberries: apple and
blackberry pie, 134
blueberries: raspberry, kiwi, and
blueberry smoothie, 14
   steamed lemon and blueberry
pudding, 137
boiled eggs, 29

bolognese sauce, 78
bread: milky white bread, 25
   spiced bread, 25
   whole wheat bread, 25
   see also flatbreads; pita
breads
broccoli: chicken and broccoli
noodles, 56
burgers, homemade, 112
butter beans: sausage and bean
soup, 70
butterflied leg of lamb, 95

C

cakes: banana cake, 130
   basic cake, 126
   carrot cake, 130
   devil's food cake, 129
   lemon polenta cake, 126
capers: tartar sauce, 119
carrots: beef and carrot
casserole, 77
   carrot, apple, and ginger
smoothie, 14
   carrot cake, 130
   carrot, chicken, and toasted
sesame pouch, 37
   charmoula, 117
   roast sesame beets, parsnips,
and carrots, 100
casseroles: beef and carrot
casserole, 77
   cassoulet, 114
   chicken and bacon pot, 106
   see also curries
cassoulet, 114
cauliflower: cauliflower with
cheese sauce, 100
   three-cheese cauliflower, 61
charmoula, 117
cheese: cauliflower with cheese
sauce, 100
   cheese dip, 40
   cheesy dumplings, 77
   ham and cheese flatbread, 34
   homemade burgers, 112
   Italian meatballs with pasta,
58
   macaroni, spinach, and
cheese bake, 74
   Parmesan and ham straws, 48
   three-cheese cauliflower, 61

tomato, basil, and mozzarella
pizza, 88
chicken: carrot, chicken, and
toasted sesame pouch, 37
   chicken and bacon pot, 106
   chicken and broccoli noodles,
56
   chicken in a pot, 103
   chicken soup, 53
   roast chicken with lemon,
thyme, and potato stuffing,
92
   Thai chicken noodle salad, 46
   Thai green chicken curry, 82
chicken livers: meatloaf with two
sauces, 111
chickpeas: lemony hummus, 40
   oven-roasted vegetables with
couscous and, 42
chili con carne, 78
chiles: harissa, 117
   hot and sour sauce, 119
   red chile sauce, 117
chocolate: chocolate swamp
pudding, 133
   devil's food cake, 129
   nutty jacks, 122
   oat and chocolate cookies,
125
   quick chocolate sauce, 138
   pear upside-down dessert,
137
   whole wheat banana and
chocolate muffins, 27
chorizo and bean pasties, 50
coconut: honeyjacks, 122
compotes, 18
cookies, 125
couscous, oven-roasted
vegetables with chickpeas
and, 42
cream cheese: carrot cake, 130
   classic smoked salmon bagel,
37
crêpes, 138
crêpe toppings, 138
crumble, almond fruit, 134
cucumber: tzatziki, 40
curries: Indian lamb curry, 82
   shrimp curry, 85
   Thai green chicken curry, 82
   vegetable curry, 85

D

devil's food cake, 129
dips, 39–40
dried fruit: granola, 21
   muesli, 21
   winter dried fruit pot, 18
drinks, 14–17
duck: cassoulet, 114
   roast duck with citrus fruits,
99
dumplings, cheesy, 77

E

eggs: boiled eggs, 29
   eggs cocotte, 30
   flat eggs, 29
   kidney bean, egg, and ham
salad, 45
   mushroom frittata, 67
   omelet, 30
   poached eggs, 29
   scrambled eggs, 31

F

fish and shrimp kedgeree,
103
fish cakes, 81
flapjacks, English, 122
flatbreads: ham and cheese
flatbread, 34
   spicy vegetable wrap, 34
flat eggs, 29
frittata, mushroom, 67
frozen berry muffins, 26
frozen berry yogurt cup, 22
fruit: almond fruit crumble, 134
   frozen berry muffins, 26
   frozen berry yogurt cup, 22
   pear upside-down dessert,
137
   seasonal fruit tray tart, 133
   see also dried fruit

G

garlic: gremolata, 118
   Mediterranean garlic shrimp,
106
gherkins: tartar sauce, 119
ginger vegetable noodles, 46
golden butternut squash soup,
70
granola, 21

banana, pecan, and granola yogurt pot, 22
gravy, 96, 100
green bean risotto, 67
green sauce, 118
gremolata, 118
guacamole, 39

H

ham: baked ham with layered potatoes, 109
ham and cheese flatbread, 34
kidney bean, egg, and ham salad, 45
meatloaf, 111
Parmesan and ham straws, 48
pasta with ham and peas, 56
pea and ham soup, 53
prosciutto-wrapped salmon on mash, 64
harissa, 117
harissa and herb dip, 39
herbs: green sauce, 118
hollandaise sauce, 116
honeyjacks, 122
hot and sour sauce, 119
hummus, lemony, 40

I

Indian lamb curry, 82
Italian meatballs, 58

K

kedgeree, fish and shrimp, 103
kidney beans: chili con carne, 78
kidney bean, egg, and ham salad, 45
kiwi fruit: raspberry, kiwi, and blueberry smoothie, 14

L

lamb: butterflied leg of lamb with Mediterranean stuffing, 95
cassoulet, 114
Indian lamb curry, 82
lamb pilaf, 86
lamb and potato pie, 74
Lancashire hotpot, 63
Lancashire hotpot, 63
lassi, mango, 17
lemon: gremolata, 118
lemon meringue pie, 141
lemon polenta cake, 126
lemony hummus, 40
steamed lemon and blueberry pudding, 137
lentil and baked tomato salad, 45
limes: hot and sour sauce, 119

M

macaroni, spinach, and cheese bake, 74
mango lassi, 17
mayo, mustard, 116
meatloaf, 111
meatballs with pasta, 58
Mediterranean garlic shrimp, 106
Mediterranean stuffing, 95
meringues: lemon meringue pie, 141
meringues with baked plums, 141
milky white bread, 25
minestrone with pesto, 73
muesli, 21
muffins, 26–7
mushrooms: chicken and bacon pot, 106
mushroom frittata, 67
vegetable, seed, and nut cakes, 81
mustard mayo, 116

N

noodles: chicken and broccoli noodles, 56
ginger vegetable noodles, 46
rice noodle salad with shrimp, 46
Thai chicken noodle salad, 46
nuts: muesli, 21
nutty jacks, 122

O

oats: English flapjacks, 122
granola, 21
honeyjacks, 122
muesli, 21
nutty jacks, 122
oat and apple muffins, 26
oat and chocolate cookies, 125
porridge, 21

omelet, 30
onions: harissa, 117
onion soup, 73

P

pancakes see crêpes
Parmesan and ham straws, 48
parsnips, roast sesame beets, carrots and, 100
pasta: Italian meatballs with pasta, 58
macaroni, spinach, and cheese bake, 74
pasta with ham and peas, 56
spaghetti bolognese, 78
pastries: chorizo and bean pasties, 50
Parmesan and ham straws, 48
sausage rolls, 49
peanuts: vegetable, seed and nut cakes, 81
pears: apple and pear compote, 18
pear upside-down dessert, 137
peas: green bean risotto, 67
pasta with ham and, 56
pea and ham soup, 53
peppers: harissa, 117
pesto, minestrone with, 73
pies: apple and blackberry pie, 134
lamb and potato pie, 74
lemon meringue pie, 141
pilaf, lamb, 86
pita breads: carrot, chicken, and toasted sesame pouch, 37
pizza: tomato, basil, and mozzarella, 88
plums: meringues with baked plums, 141
plum and honey cup, 22
rhubarb and plum compote, 18
poached eggs, 29
polenta: easy tuna patties, 64
lemon polenta cake, 126
pork: cassoulet, 114
Italian meatballs, 58
meatloaf, 111
roast pork, 96
spareribs, 86

porridge, 21
potatoes: baked ham with layered potatoes, 109
lamb and potato pie, 74
Lancashire hotpot, 63
lemon, thyme, and potato stuffing, 92
prosciutto-wrapped salmon on mash, 64
roast potatoes, 100
traditional fish cakes, 81
vegetable, seed, and nut cakes, 81
prosciutto-wrapped salmon on mash, 64
pumpkin seed cookies, 125

R

raspberry, kiwi, and blueberry smoothie, 14
red chile sauce, 117
rhubarb and plum compote, 18
rice: fish and shrimp kedgeree, 103
green bean risotto, 67
lamb pilaf, 86
rice noodle salad, 46
risotto, green bean, 67

S

salads: kidney bean, egg, and ham, 45
lentil and baked tomato, 45
rice noodle with shrimp, 46
Thai chicken noodle, 46
salmon: prosciutto-wrapped salmon on mash, 64
traditional fish cakes, 81
sauces, 116–19
charmoula, 117
chocolate sauce, 138
gravy, 96, 100
green sauce, 118
gremolata, 118
harissa, 117
hollandaise sauce, 116
hot and sour sauce, 119
mustard mayo, 116
red chile sauce, 117
spiced tomato sauce, 111
tartar sauce, 119
tomato sauce, 111

sausages: cassoulet, 114
    sausage and bacon toad-in-
        the-hole, 61
    sausage and bean soup, 70
    sausage rolls, 49
scrambled eggs, 31
seasonal fruit tray tart, 133
seeds: granola, 21
    pumpkin seed cookies, 125
    vegetable, seed, and nut
        cakes, 81
shortbread, 125
shrimp: fish and shrimp
        kedgeree, 103
    Mediterranean garlic shrimp,
        106
    shrimp curry, 85
    rice noodle salad with, 46
smoked haddock: fish and
        shrimp kedgeree, 103
smoked salmon bagel, 37
smoothies, 14–17
soups: chicken soup, 53
    golden butternut squash soup,
        70
    minestrone with pesto, 73
    onion soup, 73
    pea and ham soup, 53
    sausage and bean soup, 70
spaghetti: Italian meatballs with
        pasta, 58
    spaghetti bolognese, 78
spareribs, 86
spinach: eggs cocotte, 30
    green bean risotto, 67
    macaroni, spinach, and
        cheese bake, 74
    mushroom frittata, 67
    vegetable, seed, and nut
        cakes, 81
squash: golden butternut
        squash soup, 70
strawberry and banana
        smoothie, 17
stuffings, 92, 95
sweet potatoes: easy tuna
        patties, 64

T
tartar sauce, 119
tart, seasonal fruit tray, 133

Thai chicken noodle salad, 46
Thai green chicken curry, 82
toad-in-the-hole, sausage and
        bacon, 61
tomatoes: guacamole, 39
    Italian meatballs with pasta, 58
    lentil and baked tomato salad,
        45
    spiced tomato sauce, 111
    tomato, basil, and mozzarella
        pizza, 88
    tomato sauce, 111
tuna patties, 64
turkey: meat loaf, 111
tzatziki, 40

U
upside-down dessert, pear, 137

V
vegetables: chicken in a pot,
        103
    ginger vegetable noodles, 46
    minestrone with pesto, 73
    oven-roasted vegetables with
        chickpeas and couscous,
        42
    spicy vegetable wrap, 34
    steamed vegetables, 100
    vegetable curry, 85
    vegetable, seed, and nut
        cakes, 81

W
walnuts: carrot cake, 130
white beans: cassoulet, 114
    chorizo and bean pasties, 50
    minestrone with pesto, 73
whole wheat banana and
        chocolate muffins, 27
whole wheat bread, 25
winter dried fruit pot, 18
wrap, spicy vegetable, 34

Y
yogurt: banana, pecan, and
        granola yogurt pot, 22
    frozen berry yogurt cup, 22
    mango lassi, 17
    plum and honey cup, 22
    tzatziki, 40

conversion chart

Weights and measures have been rounded up
or down slightly to make measuring easier.

Measuring butter:

A US stick of butter weighs 4 oz. which is
approximately 115 g or 8 tablespoons. The recipes in
this book require the following conversions:

American	Metric	Imperial
6 tbsp	85 g	3 oz.
7 tbsp	100 g	3½ oz.
1 stick	115 g	4 oz.

Volume equivalents:

American	Metric	Imperial
1 teaspoon	5 ml	
1 tablespoon	15 ml	
¼ cup	60 ml	2 fl.oz.
⅓ cup	75 ml	2½ fl.oz.
½ cup	125 ml	4 fl.oz.
⅔ cup	150 ml	5 fl.oz. (¼ pint)
¾ cup	175 ml	6 fl.oz.
1 cup	250 ml	8 fl.oz.

Weight equivalents: **Measurements:**

Imperial	Metric	Inches	Cm
1 oz.	30 g	¼ inch	5 mm
2 oz.	55 g	½ inch	1 cm
3 oz.	85 g	¾ inch	1.5 cm
3½ oz.	100 g	1 inch	2.5 cm
4 oz.	115 g	2 inches	5 cm
5 oz.	140 g	3 inches	7 cm
6 oz.	175 g	4 inches	10 cm
8 oz. (½ lb.)	225 g	5 inches	12 cm
9 oz.	250 g	6 inches	15 cm
10 oz.	280 g	7 inches	18 cm
11½ oz.	325 g	8 inches	20 cm
12 oz.	350 g	9 inches	23 cm
13 oz.	375 g	10 inches	25 cm
14 oz.	400 g	11 inches	28 cm
15 oz.	425 g	12 inches	30 cm
16 oz. (1 lb.)	450 g		

Oven temperatures:

150°C	(300°F)	Gas 2
170°C	(325°F)	Gas 3
180°C	(350°F)	Gas 4
190°C	(375°F)	Gas 5
200°C	(400°F)	Gas 6